The Revelation
of God
in
Human Suffering

BOOKS BY WAYNE E. OATES

Published by The Westminster Press

The Revelation of God in Human Suffering
Where to Go for Help
Anxiety in Christian Experience
The Bible in Pastoral Care
The Christian Pastor

The Revelation
of God
in
Human Suffering

Books by Wayne E. Oates
Published by The Westminster Press

The Revelation of God in Human Suffering
Where to Go for Help
Anxiety in Christian Experience
The Bible in Pastoral Care
The Christian Pastor

The Revelation
of God
in
Human Suffering

by

WAYNE E. OATES

Philadelphia

THE WESTMINSTER PRESS

Library of Congress Catalog Card No. 59–8226

PRINTED IN THE UNITED STATES OF AMERICA

To
Gaines S. Dobbins

CONTENTS

PREFACE

IN THESE SERMONS I speak as a preacher who is committed, inasmuch as in me lies, to proclaim " the whole counsel of God." The central theme is depicted in the title, *The Revelation of God in Human Suffering*. The theme of the stresses of life aims to give a common core of meaning and continuity to the sermons that have been developed in my own preaching ministry over a period of nearly twenty years since my ordination as a preacher of the Christian gospel.

Usually a person expects me to write a book on " pastoral counseling," " pastoral psychology," or " psychology of religion." For this very reason I am publishing a book of sermons. Counseling, psychology, and psychology of religion as implemented by a Christian pastor are inseparable from the work he does as a preacher. I take as my guiding light in this task the work of Jonathan Edwards, who saw vitally the relationship between his preaching and the " religious affections of man." Therefore, he wrote his " Treatise Concerning the Religious Affections." Even at the risk of making strange bedfellows of Edwards and Horace Bushnell, I note also with interest that Horace Bushnell's profound psychological concern for developmental problems in Christian nurture breathe like sweet incense through his sermons, such as the one on " Unconscious Influence." In other words, what I am saying is that the sermon is a living testimony of psychological wisdom and not a reflective essay *about* psychology.

Furthermore, in order that I may do what I can to undermine the idea that no one reads books of sermons, I am being bold enough to publish one with my publisher's gracious assistance. The lay person in the churches, the growing student in the chapel, the person outside the churches and chapels whose main avenue to knowing God will be through the sufferings that beset him on every side — these are my audience. I am convinced that they do read books of sermons many times when they do not even go to church. I am acutely aware of the private burdens many ministers themselves carry. I hope that this book will help them both personally and as preachers themselves.

These sermons have all been preached to audiences of church people, theological seminary chapel gatherings, and congregations of religious assemblies of many different kinds. However, the spoken word and the written word are vastly different media of communication. A sermon that is spoken must be adapted to a known audience that also knows the preacher. But the written sermon goes to a reading audience who may or may not know and be known by the preacher. And, as Harry Emerson Fosdick has said, "sermons were not meant to be read, as essays are." For, as Phillips Brooks has said, preaching is essentially the communication of divine truth through human personality. Therefore, a sermon, as Fosdick says, is "direct personal address, individual consultation on a group scale, intended to achieve results. . . . If a printed sermon is to seem real, therefore, the reader must read as though he were listening." (Harry Emerson Fosdick in *On Being Fit to Live With,* p. vii. Harper & Brothers, 1946.)

Prof. J. B. Weatherspoon once said about the use of psychological concepts in preaching: " When you go into the pulpit, just take the cream with you. Don't drag the separator in too! " Even though I have spent a lot of time working in the field of pastoral psychology, Professor Weatherspoon's suggestion has been a watchword for me as I have preached and written these sermons. The art of preaching calls for concealment of the art, because it is the eternal God in Christ to whom we call attention when we preach, not art or psychology. Psychological concepts should be understood well enough by the Christian preacher that they can be a part of his preaching without obscuring his main purpose of proclamation of the Christian witness. Biblical materials should be used without the trappings of jargon and without straining the text of the Scripture.

One more thing needs to be said about the relationships between preaching and counseling. A very real difference between these two ministries of the pastor exists alongside equally important similarities. When the preacher preaches, he appeals to the common and more universal elements in the human situation, whereas the pastoral counselor is committed to discovering the unique individuality of one person at a time and what the universals mean to him. Biblical preaching helps the pastor to rise above the particularities of his counselees to the wholeness of the counsel of God for every man. The effective preacher grounds his preaching and squares and plumbs it Biblically. Thus he avoids the fate of overgeneralizing about *all* people on the basis of hasty experience with one or two people. The inexhaustible wisdom of the Scriptures is the stuff of the revelation of God for all time. The stresses and strains of human suffering bring the Scriptures into bold relief again and again to the Christian pastor who has an intimate ac-

quaintance both with the Bible and with suffering. The intention of these sermons is to weave the warp of Biblical
revelation and the woof of human suffering into a fabric
of durable Christian preaching.

WAYNE E. OATES

ACKNOWLEDGMENTS

REAL APPRECIATION is due many persons for the inspiration necessary for me to have written these pages. Simon Doniger, editor of *Pastoral Psychology,* first suggested the motif of these sermons. He generously published several of them periodically in the pages of his journal. Dr. Roland W. Tapp has carefully evaluated these materials and given helpful editorial assistance. The congregation of the First Baptist Church, Lumberton, North Carolina, listened to many of these sermons as I preached them during a spiritual life commitment week in 1957. They heard me gladly and caused me to feel that the sermons in written form would have increasing usefulness to lay people. Students in chapel services at Southern Baptist Theological Seminary and Union Theological Seminary in New York joined minds with me as I preached others of the sermons. My family has listened to some of them more than once and always acted as though they were new each time.

A special debt of gratitude is due Mrs. Joe Baskin, Miss Belva Boston, and Miss Joyce Cherry for their efficient service in typing this manuscript.

THE REVELATION OF GOD
IN HUMAN SUFFERING

When the Son of man comes in his glory, and all the angels with him, then he will sit on his glorious throne. Before him will be gathered all the nations, and he will separate them one from another as a shepherd separates the sheep from the goats, and he will place the sheep at his right hand, but the goats at the left. Then the King will say to those at his right hand, "Come, O blessed of my Father, inherit the kingdom prepared for you from the foundation of the world; for I was hungry and you gave me food, I was thirsty and you gave me drink, I was a stranger and you welcomed me, I was naked and you clothed me, I was sick and you visited me, I was in prison and you came to me." Then the righteous will answer him, "Lord, when did we see thee hungry and feed thee, or thirsty and give thee drink? And when did we see thee a stranger and welcome thee, or naked and clothe thee? And when did we see thee sick or in prison and visit thee?" And the King will answer them, "Truly, I say to you, as you did it to one of the least of these my brethren, you did it to me."

— Matt. 25:31-40.

THE audience to whom Jesus spoke had been reared on phrases like these: "No one has ever seen God." "Man shall not see me and live." The hiddenness of God was the meat and bread of their spiritual diet. What an affront it must have been, therefore, for them to hear the Christian gospel, which boldly said, "The Word became flesh and dwelt among us, full of grace and truth; we have beheld his glory, glory as of the only Son from the Father" (John 1:14)! This full revelation became the center of the Christian faith, and the writer of I John could say, "By this you know the Spirit of God: every spirit which confesses that Jesus Christ has come in the flesh is of God" (I John 4:2). He could also say with breath-taking firsthandedness of experience, "That which was from the beginning, which we have heard, which we have seen with our eyes, which we have looked upon and touched with our hands, concerning the word of life — the life was made manifest, and we saw it, and testify to it, and proclaim to you the eternal life which was with the Father and was made manifest to us — that which we have seen and heard we proclaim also to you, so that you may have fellowship with us; and our fellowship is with the Father and with his Son Jesus Christ" (I John 1:1-3).

But in the last days of the flesh of Jesus Christ, he was acutely aware that men would revert to speculation, "gazing into heaven," and to fearful anxiety in order to recover the luminous radiance of his continuing revelation of himself to them. Therefore he told them in plain words where and when he would reveal himself to them. This instruction he gave in the parable of the judging shepherd, who reveals himself daily in the suffering of needy people. The vision of the living Christ in the needs of the hungry, the thirsty, the stranger, the naked, the sick, and the imprisoned was to be henceforth his primary meeting place with his followers, and their awareness of the cries of his "little ones" would be the basis of judgment and separation, acceptance and fellowship, before God. In the sufferings of needy persons he comes upon us in fullest clarity. We do not always expect to see him most vividly here. Therefore we may be unaware of his presence. More often, in being callous to the distress of his " little ones," we may be insensitive and blind to his revelation of himself to us. But in either event, the vision of God in Christ is most vividly real in the sufferings of human personalities about us. Therefore, let us look more closely at the nature of Christ's revelation of himself to us, the character of our response to this revelation, and the ultimate meaning that this revelation has for us.

THE CONTINUING SELF-DISCLOSURE OF CHRIST

The Christ who holds the fate of the universe in his hands, both in his earthly and in his continuing disclosure of himself, has chosen to make himself known through the pangs of the hungry, the desperation of the sick, the exposure of the naked, the loneliness of the stranger, and the self-defeatedness of the prisoner. Christ continues to reveal himself anew in the extreme needs of " the least of these his brethren." In them we do not find the mere footprints and fingerprints of where he *has* been. Here we find his feet and hands themselves. Here we do not hear an echo of his voice, but the voice of the Christ himself. Here we find the Christ himself achingly involved in the destiny of human beings.

During his historic incarnation, Jesus pointed to his identity with human sufferers as evidence for the fact that the Messiah had come. John the Baptist and his followers, in true tradition with their contemporaries, needed evidence as to his Messiahship. Men for centuries had looked for the Messiah to come. They had many wild guesses as to how he would make himself known. They averred that he would come in a blinding Shekinah of light, a brilliant theophany that would cause every other light among men to cast a shadow. They also thought that he would come as a military ruler and crush by his power the oppressor under whose heel they themselves were being held in subjection. They, like many groups today, had all sorts of astrologies and date charts to determine when and how he would come, how long he would rule, and what would happen thereafter. They scanned sacred books and pitted this authority against that until students wound up in confusion or decided to take advantage of the confusion and get as much out of it for themselves as they could. Little wonder is it that when John the Baptist heard " about the deeds of the Christ, he sent word by his disciples and said to him, ' Are you he who is to come, or shall we look for another? ' "

In Jesus' reply we hear no debate, no protesting too much, no extravagant arguments, no insecurity of rejection. We hear him saying, " Go and tell John what you hear and see: the blind receive their sight and the lame walk, lepers are cleansed and the deaf hear, and the dead are raised up, and the poor have good news preached to them." These words rose to the surface of the awareness of the disciples of both John and Jesus. Underneath them was the deep-running sense of mission of the Anointed One who, strengthened by the Holy Spirit after the struggle of decision in the wilderness, made the prophecy of Isaiah fact in flesh as he preached at Nazareth and said:

> The Spirit of the Lord is upon me,
> because he has anointed me to preach good news
>   to the poor.
> He has sent me to proclaim release to the captives
> and recovering of sight to the blind,
> to set at liberty those who are oppressed,
> to proclaim the acceptable year of the Lord.
> . . . And he began to say to them, " Today this scripture
> has been fulfilled in your hearing." (Luke 4:18-19, 21.)

In his commission to his disciples, he transfused his revelation of the intention of the Father into the work of his disciples. He thrust them into active involvement with the sick, the spirit-possessed, and the deprived ones. They returned from their first assignment with their eyes glowing with the fresh vision of the reality of their Master and the strength of his compassion. They said with breathless excitement, joy, and exaltation, " Lord, even the demons are subject to us in your name! "

This triumphant ministry to the oppressed, this freeing of those bound by possessing spirits, was to Jesus an exultant revelation of the power of the Father released through him and his disciples as they gave themselves with abandon to "the least of these his brethren." He exclaimed at what he saw, " I saw Satan fall like lightning from heaven." Yet, he disciplined himself and his followers by saying to them that they were not to rejoice over the power that had coursed through their lives, subjecting demons unto them. Rather, they were to rejoice that through this ministry they were lastingly related to the Kingdom of Heaven. Then he gave thanks for the revelation of the Father to his disciples in the ministry to needy persons: " I thank thee, Father, Lord of heaven and earth, that thou hast hidden these things from the wise and understanding and revealed them to babes; yea, Father, for such was thy gracious will." (See Luke 10:17-22.)

Martin Luther caught the full thrust of Jesus' revelation of himself in the suffering of Frederick of Saxony, who fell desperately sick in September, 1519. Luther wrote a letter to his friend in the crisis of his illness and said:

> When . . . I learned . . . that Your Lordship has been afflicted with a grave illness and that Christ has at the same time become ill in you. . . I cannot pretend that I do not hear the voice of Christ crying out to me from Your Lordship's body and flesh saying, " Behold, I

am sick." This is so because such evils as illness . . . are not borne by us who are Christians but by Christ himself, our Lord and Savior, in whom we live, even as Christ plainly testifies . . . when he says, " Inasmuch as ye have done it unto one of the least of these my brethren, ye have done it unto me." (*Luther: Letters of Spiritual Counsel,* ed. by Theodore G. Tappert, p. 27. The Westminster Press, 1955.)

For those of us who are trained for the ministry of the gospel of Christ, one seriously sick person reminded us that we should not expect the revelation of God to be recorded in books and to be gathering dust upon library shelves before we sought it in earnest. Anton Boisen, out of the heated crucible of a severe mental disorder, discovered for himself and for succeeding generations of ministers that the real laboratory for discovering the clearest revelation of the meaning of God in Christ was among the sick, the outcast, the distressed failures of life. These " least ones " were, according to him, the " written, living human documents of flesh and blood " where God was most certainly making himself known.

Having had this man as a teacher, I can say as an eyewitness that he is right, because, as I have walked into hospital rooms under his supervision I have felt the living presence of the Christ and have had the meaning of his recorded words come alive to me. So much is this so that I am convinced that the shepherding ministry, to which every Christian is called and for which the pastor is specifically trained, is one of the headsprings of the ever-renewing water of life known as Christian theology. This shepherding ministry both vitalizes and purifies our knowledge of God.

Purity of Heart and the Self-disclosure of Christ

Such a ministry to suffering people as we have been talking about does not *necessarily* imply that those who minister to the needy will automatically enter into a clear revelation of Christ. The clarity of their motives, the purity of their hearts, for performing this task has much to do with this discovery. In fact, the surprising element in the parable of the judging shepherd is that Christ's disclosure of himself came sometime later — after the acts of mercy and consideration had been performed. This leads us to believe that our motives for ministering to other people must be without a great deal of self-consciousness that we are doing something special, and certainly without a conscious campaign to "get a revelation" out of this ministry.

For example, those "blessed ones of the Father" of whom Jesus spoke were not aware of being on a "quest for revelation." They had not gone there looking for a revelation. So complete was their abandon and so unconditional was their love for those for whom they cared that their left hand was unaware of what their right hand was doing. They did not do their good works to be seen of men, to see Christ, or to increase their knowledge of theology. Surprisingly enough, the "blessed ones of the Father" asked the same question as did the accursed ones: "Lord, when did we see thee . . . ?" The unawareness of the one expressed the completeness of their abandon and love in serving; the unawareness of the other expressed the callousness of their neglect of the needy.

Those who inherited the Kingdom of Christ were rewarded on the basis of their ministry, but Jesus carefully revealed that they did not set out with this reward as their objective. Theirs was a ministry to "the least of these his brethren " because of an uncomplicated love for them in and of themselves. They were ends in themselves, worthy of love in their own right, and not means to the ends of those who did things for them. Those who ministered to them went to them with " clean hands and pure hearts," with no hidden motives, no attempt to minister to personal needs to be righteous, no attempt to get something out of them or to maneuver them toward previously self-chosen ends. They were not trying to make " rice " Christians of them, that is, giving them food to get professions of faith in the Christian religion. They were not trying to get a " confession " out of them, which would both be good for their souls and satisfy the curiosity of those who went to them. They did not have to have a reason other than their nonseeking kind of love and did not take time to become highly analytical about that. Theirs was religion that was " pure and undefiled before God," and their motives were " unstained from the world."

Today we are called upon to re-examine our motives for the service of needy people. We can very easily give and give and give to a needy family without ever taking the time to investigate the reasons for the family's plight or the motives for which we help. We may easily be undercutting the initiative of the family and failing to help them to help themselves. We may easily be doing our good deeds for them just to get them off our hands and to ease our consciences rather than to take the time to come to know them as persons, to minister to them totally rather than partially.

On the other hand, we may be exceptionally eager to turn our most recent ambitions to minister to needy people into grist for our public relations departments.

The laymen of the Committee on Institutions of the Louisville Council of Churches have steadily improved the condition of the inmates of prisons, hospitals, and child-care institutions through their co-operation with the administration and staff of these agencies. However, one of the key secrets to their effectiveness is that they have discreetly avoided publicity for their more important projects. Likewise, a negative example of this may be seen in the efforts of certain communities to set up church-related counseling centers for the care of disturbed and unhappy individuals and families. One of the first mistakes such groups tend to make is to get wide newspaper publicity for their projects. But the very nature of the counseling ministry is private, anonymous, confidential, and self-erasing. Such publicity contributes to the failure of such projects, because it is the antithesis of the ministry offered. Jesus in his ministry to disturbed people sent them away with instructions to " say nothing to any one." But we advertise ours in the papers. Little wonder is it that desperate people hesitate to entrust their heart's anguish to publicity-hungry churchmen!

The Bases of Christ's Judgment

The spiraling point of Jesus' parable of the judging shepherd reaches a dramatic climax as the Son of Man pronounces the separating judgment upon the " lived lives " of those before him! Jesus lived under the tension of the acute shortness of time. The words of this parable were apparently uttered under the very shadow of the cross that would end his own life. He was forced to thresh the issues of life down to the most urgent, pressing, and demanding ones and to deal with them in these fleeting moments. He breathed upon his disciples the shortness of the present age as well as the fact that his own personal hour was close at hand. He had said to them earlier, " There are some standing here who will not taste death before they see the

Son of man coming in his kingdom " (Matt. 16:28). Now, in this parable, he described that coming, that event in eternity. He put his hands squarely upon the only issue that really mattered and held it up before them as the one issue that would balance the scales of his judgment: Hereby are we to be sure that we know him — if we keep his commandment to love our brother in the stresses of his life to the end that we will spend and be spent in his behalf without calling even our own attention to the fact.

My life and yours are being lived out under a promise of their appalling shortness. Many of the things to which we have given our lives are only peripheral to the central meaning of life. They are far afield from the core of Christ's continuing disclosure of himself. The issues over which we have been willing to bleed and let blood from others have been mere straw men compared to the poignancy of the hungry, the thirsty, the naked, the sick, and the imprisoned. We live our lives under the threat of world catastrophe and the impending cataclysmic end of the age. But when the clamor of the confusion of voices is overcome by the clarity of the voice of the Son of Man, we can say with Frank Mason North:

> Where cross the crowded ways of life,
>   Where sound the cries of race and clan,
> Above the noise of selfish strife,
>   We hear thy voice, O Son of Man!
>
> In haunts of wretchedness and need,
>   On shadowed thresholds dark with fears,
> From paths that hide the lures of greed,
>   We catch the vision of thy tears.
>
> The cup of water given for thee
>   Still holds the freshness of thy grace;

Yet long these multitudes to see
   The sweet compassion of thy face.

O Master, from the mountainside
   Make haste to heal those hearts of pain;
Among these restless throngs abide,
   O tread the city's streets again,

Till sons of men shall learn thy love,
   And follow where thy feet have trod;
Till glorious, from thy heaven above,
   Shall come the City of our God.

JESUS AND THE REALITY OF SUFFERING

Therefore, having this ministry by the mercy of God, we do not lose heart. We have renounced disgraceful, underhanded ways; we refuse to practice cunning or to tamper with God's word, but by the open statement of the truth we would commend ourselves to every man's conscience in the sight of God. And even if our gospel is veiled, it is veiled only to those who are perishing. In their case the god of this world has blinded the minds of the unbelievers, to keep them from seeing the light of the gospel of the glory of Christ, who is the likeness of God. For what we preach is not ourselves, but Jesus Christ as Lord, with ourselves as your servants for Jesus' sake. For it is the God who said, " Let light shine out of darkness," who has shone in our hearts to give the light of the knowledge of the glory of God in the face of Christ.

— II Cor. 4:1-6.

THE central fact about the revelation of God is not that you and I have sufferings in which God reveals himself to us. Rather, the core of truth in the revelation of God is that he, in Jesus Christ as Lord, has himself entered the arena of human suffering, taking upon himself the form of a servant, fashioning himself in the likeness of suffering humanity, and humbling himself to the death that is ours to bear. Thereby he effects our redemption in this historic act of becoming man in order that, as Athanasius put it, he might deify us. Paul, in the passage of Scripture quoted above, says that God has given us the light of the knowledge of himself in the face of Jesus Christ. Therefore, we do well in our search for the revelation of God in human suffering to underscore for all eternity that the suffering of Jesus Christ was the suffering of a real human being. In the face of Jesus Christ, God revealed from the foundations of the world his supreme intention for the redemption of mankind. We need, therefore, to refresh our memory of the face of Jesus Christ, for in this face is the Christian hope fully expressed.

The glow of love's idealism casts over the face of one whom we love a luminous quality that eludes the memory. Therefore we constantly hasten back again and again to the faces of those whom we love, who have suffered most for us, and from whom we draw our deepest spiritual sustenance. So it is with the face of Jesus Christ. We hasten again and again to the pages of the New Testament for a renewed vision of his face, that we may once again see the revelations of his Passion, rekindle our hearts with his love, and renew our spiritual resources by doing so.

But even in the New Testament we do not have any description of the physical appearance of Jesus. We assume that this was because of the natural aversion of the Hebrew writers to giving the reader a certain set of features of which to make an idol, icon, or image. We do not know what color his eyes and hair were; we do not know his height or weight; nor do we know anything of his complexion or facial idiosyncrasies. Consequently, people of every race can identify him with themselves, and the lame, the halt, and the blind do not feel alien to him. He is everyman's Christ.

However, the New Testament is explicitly clear as to *the character* reflected in the face of Jesus Christ, and it is unequivocal about saying that this was the very character of God revealed there. When we examine the records carefully, we see five revealing characteristics in the face of Jesus Christ.

THE OPEN FACE OF JESUS CHRIST

The Biblical writers with one accord speak of the openness, transparency, and manifest reality of the face of Jesus Christ. This was no mask of appearance that he wore. The disciples "beheld his glory," "full of grace and truth." As he prayed before them, his countenance was altered, and the brilliance of the revelation of the true God came through to them. The express image of God's character was real to them in the face of Jesus Christ. Nevertheless, his face was a real, human face. They resisted every attempt of the early heretics of the Christian community to teach that the fleshly incarnation of Jesus Christ was not real, that it was only an appearance. They said that the person who believed that he had in reality come in the flesh was born of God, and that the person who did not believe this was not born of God. To them the reality, sincerity, and freedom from sham of the revelation of God in the face of Jesus Christ was the hallmark of their faith.

The person you see in Jesus Christ is the person that he is. The outwardly appearing and inwardly real person are the same. " The light of the knowledge of the glory of God " in his face has no variableness or shadow of turning. It is free of duplicity, sham, and deception. The personality of Jesus was not a *persona,* a mask, which he wore, but the reality that he essentially was. He was not the principal actor in a drama, but the central Person of life itself; not a dramatic reproduction of anyone, but the Person of God himself.

The apostle Paul applied this to his own preaching ministry when he said, " We have renounced disgraceful, underhanded ways; we refuse to practice cunning or to tamper with God's word, but by the open statement of the truth we would commend ourselves to every man's conscience in the sight of God." If his gospel was going to be veiled, hidden, distorted, or obscured, someone else would have to do it, because he was, in his acknowledgment of God in the face of Jesus Christ, finished with sham, deception, double talk, and duplicity. Anne Morrow Lindbergh illustrates this very clearly in her book *The Gift from the Sea* when she says:

> I find I am shedding hypocrisy in human relationships. What a rest that will be! The most exhausting thing in life, I have discovered, is being insincere. That is why so much of social life is exhausting; one is wearing a mask. I have shed my mask. (P. 32. Pantheon Books, 1955.)

Such was the injunction of Jesus to his disciples when he said, " And when you fast, do not look dismal, like the hypocrites, for they disfigure their faces that their fasting may be seen by men." Their religion was a mask of appearance. Today, men's irreligion is often a mask of appearance to obscure that profound dedication they really do feel, lest men think them to be religious in any sense of the word. This is another way of appearing to be something other than we essentially are, and has been named the new hypocrisy of the twentieth century — appearing more irreligious than we really are. A *New Yorker* cartoon sagaciously pinpointed this wisdom: one prisoner in a penitentiary yard was remarking to another prisoner as a third proudly walked by, " I just can't stand that guiltier-than-thou look of his! " Let us have done with our shams!

The Set Face of Jesus Christ

In the second place, the face of Jesus Christ is a set, a purposive, a resolved, face. In Luke 9:51 we read that " when the days drew near for him to be received up, he set his face to go to Jerusalem." He had come through the decisions in the wilderness, the threatenings of his popularity, the thrill of seeing people healed and restored to life. Now he was faced with the crucial decision of his spiritual pilgrimage: Should he go to Jerusalem? To do so was to seal his own doom, to make certain the crucifixion, to fulfill the approaching sacrifice that was his to make. But we know that, without equivocation, haggling, or indecision, he set his face steadfastly, as hard as flint, to go to Jerusalem. He had, as had the Roman legions of Caesar, " crossed the Rubicon," and there was no turning back. He had come to what the trans-Atlantic and trans-Pacific airmen call " the point of no return."

Jesus had come to the point of commitment that inevitably would lead to the cross, the grave, and the resurrection. He therefore was filled with resolve, clarity of direction, and his set face reflected this to his disciples. From him they drew later the same kind of resolve that enabled them to drink of the cup of which he then drank.

As you and I contemplate this " set " face, we have revealed to us all our own indecisiveness, our mixture of motives, our lack of clarity, and our confusion in our sense of direction. We sense the need for that simplicity of life which comes from willing one thing and which is our dedication to Christ, who " for the joy that was set before him endured the cross." As the trail blazer of our faith, his set face revealed the purpose of God for our redemption.

The Silent Face of Jesus Christ

The clarity of purpose and set sense of direction in the mind of Jesus was evidenced by a serene silence that struck astonishment in the hearts of even his accusers. We read in Matt. 27:12-14:

> But when he was accused by the chief priests and elders, he made no answer. Then Pilate said to him, " Do you not hear how many things they testify against you? " But he gave him no answer, not even to a single charge; so that the governor wondered greatly.

Men's defensiveness and need to justify their behavior appear in anxious, long-winded talkativeness. The weaker our case is the more we have to talk to relieve our own anxiety and to bolster the weaknesses of our position. In fact, this kind of chattering is often mistaken for erudition, cleverness, and a mastery of the human language. But, as Sören Kierkegaard has said, we cannot chatter our way into the Kingdom of God. The antithesis of this is seen in the face of Jesus Christ. In the presence of his accusers and under questioning from the Roman governor, Pilate, he was silent. The long, awesome, painful, and spirit-revealing silence was more than Pilate could bear. As if shattered by the break-through of the Eternal in the face of Jesus, he almost pleaded with him to say something. But Jesus answered not a word, not even to a single charge.

Was this a proud silence in which he felt himself too good to answer such charges? Was it a surly silence in which he rebuked them with his nonretaliative resistance? Was this a detached silence in which he was actually in an unreal world, one different from that which he really faced with its threat of imminent death? Was this an indecisive silence in which he simply did not know what to say if he had wanted to speak? No! It was none of these kinds of silence. This silence of Jesus was the serene silence of the Son of God, who had, through the long watches of prayer in the night, come to a clear-eyed consciousness of the central purpose of his life, the reason for which he had come into the world, and the essential identity that the Father had conferred upon him. Therefore, he could, knowing who he was and where he was going, face tragedy with serene silence that radiated hope.

THE SUFFERING FACE OF JESUS CHRIST

The New Testament writers faithfully etch the face of Jesus Christ into our memories as a suffering face. The pangs of hunger filled his face in the wilderness as he was tempted to transform stones into bread. The tears of grief stained his weather-beaten countenance as he came to the grave of his friend Lazarus. The sorrow of separation filled his face as he contemplated leaving his disciples at the Last Supper. In the hour of tension in Gethsemane his troubled countenance was evidence of his desire that the suffering be ended. Later, the soldiers pushed thorns into his head and forehead, and his face undoubtedly was streaked with blood. The face of Jesus was a suffering face.

The character of God was revealed sublimely in the suffering face of Jesus Christ. The light of the knowledge of God of our condition as sufferers was made manifest here. The identification of God with our plight as sinners was revealed here. The awareness of God of our inability to redeem ourselves, to find our own way, or to chart our own course was revealed in the suffering face of Jesus Christ.

The astounding unbelievableness of this suffering fills the Christian believer with such awe that he thinks of himself as an unbeliever. As the man cried to Jesus, so he cries, " I believe; help my unbelief! " Similarly a woman who had been divorced several times, whose eyesight was practically gone, and whose mother was at the point of death said to me: " I can believe that Christ died for the sins of all mankind, and that he is the Savior of the world. But when I look upon what a mess I have made of my life, I cannot

understand or believe how he could have suffered for me."
This is the characteristic of unsearchableness in the suffering
of Jesus Christ for the sins of mankind, and we cannot
stretch our imaginations far enough to grasp its magnitude.
The gasping sense of wonder that filled the apostle Paul
takes hold of us: " O the depth of the riches and wisdom
and knowledge of God! How unsearchable are his judg-
ments and how inscrutable his ways! " (Rom. 11:33).

THE TRANSFORMING FACE OF JESUS CHRIST

The transparent openness, the steadfast purposiveness, the
serene silence, and the self-giving suffering of the face of
Jesus Christ all combine to make his countenance a *transforming* face. We are changed into his likeness as we worship the Lord Jesus Christ. We live in the cherished hope
that we shall be in his likeness. Paul says in II Cor. 3:12-13,
16, 18:

> Since we have such a hope, we are very bold, not like
> Moses, who put a veil over his face so that the Israelites
> might not see the end of the fading splendor. . . . But
> when a man turns to the Lord the veil is removed. . . .
> And we all, with unveiled face, beholding the glory of
> the Lord, are being changed into his likeness from one
> degree of glory to another; for this comes from the Lord
> who is the Spirit.

The psychologists have a law that they call " identification." Simply stated, this law says that quite unconsciously
we become like that which we love and are changed into the
image of the object of our adoration. When we give ourselves in worship of the Lord Jesus Christ, his likeness
changes us into a new being. Old things are passed away
and all things become new. We can say with the apostle
Paul that we " have been crucified with Christ "; neverthe-

less we live; yet not we but Christ lives in us. We can ex-
claim with the writer of I John 3:1-3:

> See what love the Father has given us, that we should
> be called children of God; and so we are. . . . It does
> not yet appear what we shall be, but we know that when
> he appears we shall be like him, for we shall see him as
> he is. And everyone who thus hopes in him purifies him-
> self as he is pure.

This is true because the face of Jesus Christ is a transforming face. We can never be the same again after having once
clearly seen the " light of the knowledge of the glory of
God in the face of Christ." We shall always be different.
If, indeed, we invest our faith in him, we shall be like him,
for we shall see him as he is.

CHAPTER

3

PURPOSEFUL SUFFERING

In the days of his flesh, Jesus offered up prayers and supplications, with loud cries and tears, to him who was able to save him from death, and he was heard for his godly fear. Although he was a Son, he learned obedience through what he suffered; and being made perfect he became the source of eternal salvation to all who obey him, being designated by God a high priest after the order of Melchizedek.

— Heb. 5:7-10.

Blessed be the God and Father of our Lord Jesus Christ, the Father of mercies and God of all comfort, who comforts us in all our affliction, so that we may be able to comfort those who are in any affliction, with the comfort with which we ourselves are comforted by God. For as we share abundantly in Christ's sufferings, so through Christ we share abundantly in comfort too.

— II Cor. 1:3-5.

WHEN Albert Schweitzer said that the world is mysteriously full of suffering, he expressed the universally human sense of query, wonder, and mystery as to the meaning of suffering. Suffering that has meaning is bearable; in fact, it may even be entered into with joy. This was true of the suffering of the Lord Jesus Christ, " who for the joy that was set before him endured the cross." Throughout his ministry a sense of defined purpose in his travail of soul pervaded his whole pilgrimage with eternal meaning.

35

Yet, average, even nominal, and sometimes devout Christians search in vain for any moving purpose for the sufferings they are called upon to bear. They cannot, with all the scanning of the inscrutable darkness of their pain, find any " rhyme or reason " for it. In the presence of physical illness or handicap, they ask, " Why must I suffer this way? " When struck by grief, they ask, " Why did this have to happen to me? " They may even quite legitimately rail out against God for his mistreatment of them. More often than this, they may shrink back from the sheer size of the task of finding any meaning at all in human suffering, thereby denying themselves the revelation of God in their suffering. In numbness and apathy they live out their days. They may settle for the solution of the stoic, who simply grins and bears his pain. Or they may adopt the Oriental wisdom of Sakini in the play *The Teahouse of the August Moon,* when he said:

> Pain makes men think.
> Thought makes men wise.
> Wisdom makes life endurable.

But in either event, they miss the purpose with which God in Christ endows the vocation of human suffering with his divine calling. In search of such a calling of God, the prophets and the apostles came to grips with the purpose of their suffering. Therefore, in the Biblical witness, we find clear guidance as to the meaning of suffering.

SUFFERING AS OBEDIENCE

The Biblical witness insists that one of the main purposes of human suffering is instruction in obedience — obedience to the fact that we are men and not God — obedience to our human limitations — obedience to the discipline of humanity from which none of us can expect to be exempt and live truthfully before God. Such was the experience of Jesus in the wilderness. Here he brought himself into subjection to the limitations of his humanity in ways that most of us seek to avoid from birth. He refused to take the short cuts that would have given quick and easy gratification of his hungers. He, like Moses before him, chose to suffer affliction with the people of God rather " than to enjoy the fleeting pleasures of sin." He refused to subvert the purposes of the Kingdom of God into a political power spectacle. He refused to seek exemption from the laws of the universe which he himself had created. As the Letter to the Hebrews puts it, " although he was a Son, he learned obedience through what he suffered " (Heb. 5:8).

One of the marks of a spiritually mature person is his ability to learn from his own experience, to profit from the things that happen to him. He, like Jacob, wrestles at every River Jabbok until God breaks through the veil of mystery wrapped about his suffering and bestows a blessing, a revelation upon him. His selfhood undergoes a transformation. He is borne out of the experience into the daylight of a new sense of identity under God, even though he carries with him the scars of the struggle. Without this courage to learn obedience through the things that we suffer, we come out of our pain, not with scars, but with open and running sores of infection which infect and subvert the purposes of our total being. But with such an intention to learn from suffering, we can, as the apostle Paul says, "rejoice in our sufferings, knowing that suffering produces endurance, and endurance produces character, and character produces hope, and hope does not disappoint us, because God's love has been poured into our hearts through the Holy Spirit which has been given to us " (Rom. 5:3-5).

However, one of the marks of a truly psychopathic person is his inability to learn from experience, or to learn obedience by the things that he suffers. He makes the same mistakes again and again. He has little or no awareness of the kinship of his troubles one to another. He considers himself an exception to all the laws of life and society. He, strangely enough, imputes to his own cleverness the power to transcend the ordinary demands of human life. His feelings of omnipotence occasionally burst forth in his treatment of other people and he is in real trouble with his brethren. When temporarily in danger of being completely isolated, rejected, and punished, he may have a superficial surge of regret that he is as he is. However, when the immediate danger of such isolation, rejection, and punishment is gone, he makes the same mistakes again, with little or no memory of having made them the first time.

In turn, this person is a source of much suffering to other people. They pay the toll of his inability to learn from experience, to take upon himself the disciplines of life, the limitations of his own humanity, and the responsibilities of corporate existence with other people. Christians so penalized may feel themselves totally responsible for this person who refuses to learn obedience. In turn, they may completely misuse human kindness and misinterpret Christian charity. By doing so, they deprive this person of the privilege of profiting from his own mistakes, protect him from his self-incurred sufferings, and misrepresent the reality of human life to him in the process. The inalienable right of every human being is to profit by his own experience. Yet in a culture such as our own, where we overprotect one another to the point of deception, we often cheat one another out of the right to suffer from our own mistakes.

Such was the experience of Jacob, again, at Jabbok. He

had deceived his father, tricked his brother, outtraded his uncle, and exploited his mother's doting love. Now he was returning to face again some of these people from whom he thought that he could flee. But Jacob himself was the one person from whom he could not flee, and the eternal God chose to confront him within the labyrinthine ways of his own spirit. He thrust him into a wrestling of soul that kept him awake in struggle all night. Such anguish and suffering often accompanies that dread moment when we stand alone before God.

Both Jacob and we ourselves can thank God that no one came to Jacob's rescue and protected him from the real anxiety that became his teacher. No one hindered the noise of the struggle in the long watches of the night. No one denied him the privilege of learning from the things that he suffered. Consequently Jacob changed. Jacob was no longer the one who had " supplanted," but Israel, the one who had " striven " with God. As such he became the namesake of the people of God. Otherwise, he would simply have been a clever " operator " on the run the rest of his life.

In contemporary life, the pastoral counselor often sees mothers and fathers who, in order to keep from being embarrassed themselves, protect their children from the consequences of their wrong behavior. The pampered child of privileged parents is often denied the right of suffering the consequences of his first brush with the law. He, therefore, begins to assume that he can " get by with anything " and the " folks will spring him." Likewise, the alcoholic is given one " out " after another by his family until he becomes totally irresponsible through the use of alcohol. The wife removes economic responsibility from him by supporting him. The father and/or mother delivers him a lecture and

pays the drunken-driving costs. But the most creative thing
they all could do for him would be to let him learn from
his own experience even if it embarrasses all of them to
tears. Then he would have something by which to remember his mistakes. Such is the hardy realism of those who
belong to Alcoholics Anonymous in their rather abrupt way
of talking and dealing with their fellow alcoholics.

The purpose of less antisocial kinds of suffering is quite
often instructional also. As one heart patient told me, the
days before his heart attack were so filled with activity
that he had forgotten how to lie down and rest. But through
his illness he had been taught his limitations and " made to
lie down " and depend upon the Good Shepherd to care
for many of the things that he, prior to his illness, felt depended completely upon himself. God reveals himself as
God in the dramatic unveiling of our humanity to us in the
experiences of illness. Often this revelation is accompanied
by great feelings of distance from God, because his greatness
and our finiteness become awesomely contrasted with each
other in the time of excruciating pain. But nevertheless, the
person who is able to learn obedience through what he
suffers becomes all the more acutely aware of his utter dependence upon God in the revelation of the " eternal quali-
tative difference between God and man " which may ac-
company a severe illness.

SUFFERING AS STEWARDSHIP

The New Testament is most vividly clear as to the purpose of suffering, however, in those places where suffering
becames an instrument of comfort, witness, and ministry
of which the sufferer is the steward. The apostle Paul makes
this transparent in his conviction that God is " the Father
of mercies and God of all comfort, who comforts us in all

our affliction." The purpose of God's comfort, in addition to teaching us through our own sufferings, is *in order that we may become a comfort to those in any affliction*. The means of our comforting of them is our own treasure of experience as a sufferer who has been comforted of God. As Robertson says: "Paul here gives the purpose of affliction in the preacher's life, in any other Christian's life, to qualify him for ministry to others. Otherwise it will be professional and perfunctory. . . . Personal experience of God's comfort is necessary before we can pass it on to others." (A. T. Robertson, in *Word Pictures in the New Testament,* Vol. IV, p. 209. The Southern Baptist Sunday School Board.)

You have been in a particularly trying time of your life and sensed that some friend of yours understood your whole situation without your having to explain that to him or her at all. A tacit sense of having been understood, appreciated, ministered unto, and comforted comes to you from that person's direction. In almost an uncanny way you have been "met," strengthened, and given hope by the very presence of that person. The chances are strong that this person has had the same trouble as or one similar to your own. Especially is this true of bereaved persons. The person who has been comforted of God in a grief of his own is thereby equipped to become a comfort to another bereaved person in a unique way.

Here, therefore, in the above passage of the apostle Paul is found the main meaning and transforming purpose of human suffering. That very suffering and God's comfort in it become a vital stewardship to be rendered to others who are in any affliction. When Anton Boisen wandered through what he called the " wilderness " of his mental illness, he began to search for the purpose of his suffering.

He found that purpose in his discovery of the suffering of his fellow patients. He dramatically laid hold of the controlling purpose of a long and useful life as a mental hospital chaplain. He became the founder of the movement for the training of ministers who would understand the struggles of mental patients as being the search for salvation and the encounter with sin. With the comfort wherewith God comforted him in his own illness, Anton Boisen became a comfort to countless thousands of other mentally ill patients through his own direct ministry and even more so through the ministry of his many students.

Jesus gave this same reassurance to the apostle Peter in advance when he predicted to him that he would be tempted and that he would crumple under the stress of temptation. But then he later told him that when he had turned and been converted, he should in turn strengthen the other disciples. We often look upon the weaknesses of the apostle Peter without taking into consideration the fact that the Lord Jesus Christ comforted him in his temptation and denial. After he had done so, he used the bitterly achieved experience of Peter to strengthen the other disciples. The apostle Peter could rightly say with the psalmist that " the bones which the Lord had broken " could rejoice because God had " hidden his face from his sins and blotted out all his iniquities."

But the author of the Letter to the Hebrews again gives us the supreme example in Jesus of the purpose of suffering wrought out in the stewardship of the comfort of God. He says that the Lord Jesus Christ learned obedience through what he suffered. In him we have a high priest who is able " to sympathize with our weaknesses." He is " one who in every respect has been tempted as we are, yet without sinning." He, " being made perfect " through his suffering, has become "the source of eternal salvation to all who obey him." Our comfort, our salvation, our hope — all these are the purpose of the suffering of Him who calls us to participation with him in the fellowship of suffering and the ministry of the word of the comfort of God.

THE FELLOWSHIP OF SUFFERING

Have this mind among yourselves, which you have in Christ
Jesus, who, though he was in the form of God, did not count
equality with God a thing to be grasped, but emptied himself,
taking the form of a servant, being born in the likeness of men.
And being found in human form he humbled himself and became obedient unto death, even death on a cross. Therefore
God has highly exalted him and bestowed on him the name
which is above every name, that at the name of Jesus every
knee should bow, in heaven and on earth and under the earth,
and every tongue confess that Jesus Christ is Lord, to the
glory of God the Father.

—Phil. 2:5-11.

LONELINESS is the aching heart of suffering. The killing
part of suffering is the way in which it cuts one off from
"the land of the living." The solitariness of our pain centers us in ourselves. It hides us from the face of the living
God. It makes our communion with one another all the
more difficult and all the more poignantly necessary. Jean-
Paul Sartre has written a starkly realistic play called *No
Exit*. He strikingly portrays three people in hell. All three
of them are trapped in an exitless room. They are incapable
of communing with or of communicating their distress to
one another. This is hell. The opposite of this is portrayed
in the meaning of suffering as set forth in the New Testament. Here, suffering is always set within a nourishing

fellowship with Christ and fellow believers in the household of faith. We need to explore some of the deeper reaches of this fellowship. In the midst of the company of the household of faith, God is always revealing himself to us as we participate in the sufferings of Christ and share with one another our mutual burdens.

THE COVENANT OF SUFFERING

The very covenant upon which the Christian faith is built centers in the sufferings of Jesus Christ. We are bound together as a community of believers in the sacrifice of his death, burial, and resurrection. The Christian confession of Jesus Christ as Lord is rooted and grounded in his self-emptying love, wrought out in his sacrificial death and perfected in the Father's exaltation of his name above every name. His obedience unto death, even the death of the cross, forms the matrix of the covenant. Without this covenant the fellowship of Christians would be merely a mutual protective association in the presence of sure destruction instead of the comradeship in the hope of the resurrection that it is. This prompted the apostle Paul to say that he did not have a righteousness of his own. His righteousness issued from the covenant faith in Christ. This covenant brought him into the arena of Christ's own sufferings and challenged him to participate in the sufferings as well as to lay hold of the promises of the resurrection.

Inevitably the acceptance of the covenant of the fellowship in Christ's sufferings issues in a disciplined relationship between those who trust wholeheartedly in the forgiving grace of God afforded by Christ in this covenant. This disciplined relationship between believers in Christ is the church itself, an organism vitalized by the Holy Spirit, the body of Christ himself.

THE FELLOWSHIP OF SIN AND FORGIVENESS

The church is not a gathering of perfect people. To the contrary, the church is made up of people who have been overwhelmed by the fact that they are sinners desperately in need of forgiveness. If we are not able to forgive our fellow man of his sins, it is firsthand evidence that we are carrying an unresolved and unconfessed, an unrecognized and unforgiven, burden of sin and guilt of our own. The covenant of suffering in Christ either has not been formed at all or has been imperfectly or only superficially begun. Paul, therefore, says that the household of faith is a burden-sharing fellowship. He says: " Brethren, if a man is overtaken in any trespass, you who are spiritual should restore him in a spirit of gentleness. Look to yourself, lest you too be tempted."

Here Paul underscores the way in which Christians bear one another's burdens and so fulfill the law of Christ. That law is the forgiveness of one another as he has forgiven us. This forgiveness is not a sentimental overlooking or glossing over of real wrongdoing, because each man is expected to accept his fair share of responsibility. The seemingly contradictory injunctions are set side by side: " Bear one another's burdens. . . . Each man will have to bear his own load." But they are merely paradoxical, not contradictory. There can be no forgiveness without real confession of fault one to another in order that healing may really take place. This calls for accepting personal responsibility for our own weaknesses at the same time as we overtake others in fault. This mutual burden-bearing is a fellowship of suffering, stripped of pretense and subterfuge and superficial claims of perfection. For " all have sinned and fall short of the glory of God " in the fellowship of sin and forgiveness we know as the church.

INDIVIDUALS UNDER GOD

A real fellowship does not come to pass by accident. A person is not capable of responsible fellowship with others who has not achieved a clear-eyed individuality under God. Being a person in one's own right is a prerequisite of a lasting fellowship with others. Martin Buber says that efforts at community that do not affirm the personhood of the individual are not fellowships of people; they are merely the collecting of people together. Herein lies one difference between the Christian and the communistic understandings of community. The one aims at the enrichment and diversity of individuality; the other, at snuffing out personal selfhood. Paul could say that he had been crucified with Christ; nevertheless he lived; yet not he but Christ lived in him. (Gal. 2:20.) He was identified with Christ, but he had not lost his personal selfhood in the process. The Christ was being lived out through his selfhood.

I am committed to a vital spiritual fellowship of all Christians. However, I must confess to a purposeful resistance to those interpretations of ecumenicity which snuff out individuality and ignore real differences of basic belief. We do not really commune with one another or learn from one another as long as we insist that each of us be a mirror of another without alteration. We easily become single-issue personalities, for instance, and judge others to be Christian or not in terms of a position taken today that will certainly change day after tomorrow. Impatience with this must have been what prompted Dostoevsky to assail the idolatry of sameness when he said:

> For these pitiful creatures are concerned . . . to find something that all would believe in and worship; what is essential is that all may be *together* in it. This craving for *community* of worship is the chief misery of every

man individually and of all humanity from the beginning of time. For the sake of common worship they've slain each other with the sword. They have set up gods and challenged one another, " Put away your gods and come and worship ours, or we will kill you and your gods! " (*The Brothers Karamazov,* tr. by Constance Garnett, p. 263. The Modern Library, Inc., 1937.)

The subtly deceptive character of evil sardonically expresses itself in those who would make an orthodoxy of ecumenicity and use it as a basis for excluding others! This is how a cause, prompted by the motives of community itself, may easily become an idolatrous crusade that further divides the community and defeats its own avowed purposes.

THE IMPULSE TO SHARE

Another cardinal feature of the Christian fellowship is the impulse to share. The Ananias who considers that he can get along without the community has not really entered it. Let's face it. The isolate who feels that it is wrong to depend upon others and who considers self-sufficiency a virtue has deprived himself of the nature of the community. The self-appointed leader who feels so weak that he has to create a self-led power structure within the group is defending his lack of selfhood. He is not opening himself to share that which he has with others. The group-chosen leader who feels self-sufficient and cannot share his leadership and so communicate his deep need of them is thereby betraying his own lack of selfhood too. Paul felt this keenly in his dependence upon some of the churches for support and his resolute intention to remain independent of others. He, therefore, in this context could say, " Let him who is taught the word share all good things with him who teaches."

Dietrich Bonhoeffer, a German Christian, was executed

by special order of Heinrich Himmler on April 9, 1945, shortly before the concentration camp in which he was imprisoned was liberated by the Allied forces. His writings "throb with the simple, downright faith of one who has met Jesus Christ and accepted the ultimate consequences of that encounter." Out of the fellowship of suffering in the dark necessities of a concentration camp, Dietrich Bonhoeffer wrote his little book, *Life Together*. In it he says that the Christian community is a gift of God which we cannot call our own. This community is not just a matter of people's feeling toward one another, but essentially the intention of God for our lives. Therefore, he says:

> Just as the Christian should not be constantly feeling his spiritual pulse, so, too, the Christian community has not been given to us by God for us to be constantly taking its temperature. The more thankfully we daily receive what is given to us, the more surely and steadily will fellowship increase and grow from day to day. (*Life Together,* p. 30. Harper & Brothers, 1954.)

This gift of God is the basis of the Christian's witness to others who would become a part of the Christian community. He declares to them what God in Christ has done for him, " so that they may fellowship with us."

Sharing is much more than the division of property. It involves the communication of the experience of older persons to younger ones, the participation of the unskilled with the more skilled, the consideration of one's achievements as those of the community and not merely one's own self-sufficient accomplishments. Sharing implies the opening of selves to one another in trust and confidence. It precludes the closing of selves to one another in suspicion and paranoid projection of blame upon one another. Sharing calls for making room for one another in our hearts, even when

we are vastly different. And sharing involves the capacity
to receive as well as to give, which is a lost art in our " do
it yourself " culture. Each one of us tends to expect himself
to be so clever that he does not need to receive another's
help. Sharing is a gift of the grace of God, disciplined
through the skills of the Christian fellowship, and taught as
a part of the culture of every growing family within the
fellowship.

An ancient story tells of the man who died and went both
to heaven and to hell. He visited hell and saw that all present were just as they had been on earth except that they
had elbows that would not bend even an inch. As he visited
heaven he found exactly the same situation. The people
were just as they had been on earth except that they had
elbows that would not bend one inch. He could not tell
any difference, therefore, between heaven and hell until he
saw the denizens of each place seated at the table trying to
eat. Here the dramatic difference appeared. In hell, the stiff-
elbowed people were in turmoil, knocking one another over
the head and unable to eat because each one was trying to
feed himself. In heaven, great joy and communion was
everywhere because each person with stiff elbows fed the
person across the table from him and vice versa! The capacity to depend and be dependent upon often makes the
difference between heaven and hell.

One of the first things I notice about the majority of the
persons who come to me in times of acute suffering seeking
personal help with their problems is the protective wall of
mistaken feelings that stands between them and anyone who
would help them bear their burdens. They almost without
exception feel guilty about needing help with their problems and sufferings. They must be reassured that suffering
is the common lot of all of us and that the heart of the

Christian community lies in mutual burden-bearing in the name of Christ. They also tend to feel that in some way or another their faith is a failure if they cannot successfully bear their troubles all by themselves. Yet this self-sufficiency itself may be close to the causal stem of some of the troubles they are having. Especially in the marital sphere, a serious hindrance to marital effectiveness is the inability of marital partners to communicate a sure sense of being needed to their partners. When, therefore, we can successfully create a fellowship in which the responsibility and the pain can be mutually borne, God breaks through with his healing help. Both pastor and parishioner begin to participate in the "fellowship of suffering" for the sheer reason of having responded to the impulse to share.

THE INTENTION OF DURABILITY

The Christian fellowship is no temporary affair of the heart between folks who want to "use" one another and then "have done" with one another. No! The Christian fellowship was intended from the foundation of the world in Christ and is to be extended from everlasting to everlasting. It is a durable communion of folks who care too deeply to want to get rid of one another. Other associations are established upon finite and temporary needs of men. The Christian fellowship is founded upon a man's ultimate needs and concerns. The people to whom he is related here are not persons whom he can treat lightly, indiscreetly, or irreverently. He will meet them again and again and again. His capacity to establish and maintain durable relationships, which is the main earthly source of strain and stress for people, is taxed to the utmost in the Christian fellowship. This is one of the main reasons why conflicts are so much more intense in a religious community when they do occur.

Paul, again, says that we live according to the dependable laws of consequences. "Whatever a man sows, that he will also reap." Then he says that to sow to the flesh is to reap that which is corruptible, perishing, temporary, transient. Sowing to the Spirit is to reap that which is incorruptible, lasting, durable, eternal. The real decisions that have to be made during times of stress are drawn along the lines of a choice between the transient and the eternal, the perishing and the lasting. The Christian fellowship always lives each moment as if it were eternity, for in its depths it actually is.

The durable hope of the Christian community is symbolized in the beatific vision of the New Jerusalem. Here the fellowship of suffering is translated into a lasting fellowship of comfort. Here, in unbroken fellowship with man, God has made his intimate dwelling with us. Bereavement is done away with, for there will be no death. God himself wipes away every tear from our eyes. Pain, mourning, crying — these symptoms of suffering will be no more. This transformation of suffering into triumph is the durable hope that binds together the Christian community.

THE STRUGGLE FOR MATURITY

When I was a child, I spoke like a child, I thought like a child, I reasoned like a child; when I became a man, I gave up childish ways.

— I Cor. 13:11.

Therefore let us leave the elementary doctrines of Christ and go on to maturity, not laying again a foundation of repentance from dead works and of faith toward God, with instruction about ablutions, the laying on of hands, the resurrection of the dead, and eternal judgment.

— Heb. 6:1-2.

Rather, speaking the truth in love, we are to grow up in every way into him who is the head, into Christ, from whom the whole body, joined and knit together by every joint with which it is supplied, when each part is working properly, makes bodily growth and upbuilds itself in love.

— Eph. 5:15-16.

THE struggle for maturity entails more suffering than do most of our momentary afflictions. Our capacity to learn from them, to discern the workings of the mind of God in stress situations, and to lay hold of the maturing resources of God's grace in these momentary situations largely depends upon our accrued maturity in Christ. The struggle for maturity is, at the heart of its meaning, the thrust of the total person in the ceaselessly changing and growing experience of relating oneself abidingly to other people and to God. The process of building mature relationships to God and to our community is another way of saying that through the divine gift of God's love we are initially enabled *to begin* to participate in the Kingdom of God. God lays the foundation of the building of mature relationships to himself and others by first having loved us in Jesus Christ our Lord. He touches us in our infirmities and quickens us in our incapacities; he perceives our low estimates of ourselves and discerns the impediments of our character that hinder us from loving him and one another with abandon and wholehearted passion, unsullied by lust. Mature relationships do not come to pass by lifting ourselves by the bootstraps of self-effort. Mature relationships are activated out of the heart of God himself in that he valued us in a way we could never have valued ourselves: he so loved us that he gave himself for us.

The love of God as the beginning and end of mature relationships is set forth in the thirteenth chapter of First Corinthians. Here the perfect love of God, the necessity for mature relationships to God and to one another, and the different kinds of immaturity among growing Christians are all set forth.

First, let us look at the different kinds of immaturity among growing Christians. Secondly, the supreme criterion of spiritual maturity, love, as the heart of interpersonal relationships needs consideration. Finally, the practical ways in which this maturity expresses itself in interpersonal living will be given attention.

The Christian, having encountered the love of God and having entered the Christian life, is, nevertheless, still involved in spiritual immaturities of various kinds. The " if's " of I Cor. 13:1-3 depict four types of spiritual immaturity.

Spiritual Articulation

The first immaturity is that stage of spiritual growth which I choose to call *the articulation and explanation of the remarkable change that has occurred in one's inner being.* The early Christians, like many of us, were in many instances uneducated and unlettered persons when they entered the Christian life. They could not find words to describe their feelings. The message of the new being in Christ burned within them and sought expression in words lest it consume them with its intensity. Some of them were so overcome with its power that they could only babble like an infant. They burst forth in unknown tongues, with no language but a cry. Yet those who also had become Christians could understand through subverbal communication that which their spiritual kinsmen were trying to utter. Paul cautioned his converts, however, to work at the business of making themselves clearly understood, lest outsiders and unbelievers consider them mad. Five words with a clear understanding are more instructive than ten thousand words in a tongue. (I Cor. 14:24 and 19, respectively.)

Men like Apollos were eloquent and spoke with much smoothness and power of oratory. Paul saw "cliques" of Christians go off after Apollos, and was quite aware of the fact that he himself did not speak in "lofty words of wisdom" (I Cor. 2:1). He saw that many of the Corinthian Christians had become fixated at this level of spiritual maturity and had become involved in speaking "in the tongues of men and of angels." As they became so fixated, they were more and more immature as time went on.

Even so, you and I get the impression too often that the person who can *say* his gospel most beautifully is *therefore* the most mature. We tend to judge ourselves and others by our ability to speak of the gospel.

Now speech is the life line of our communication with one another. It is here that counseling and healing begin: in the articulation of feeling and communication. We must, therefore, never cease to work at the business of devising ways of making ourselves understood to one another. Much of our irritability, our impatience, our rudeness, and our rejoicing when others go wrong comes of our plain inability to make ourselves understood to others. Our stubborn unwillingness to discipline ourselves to hear what they have to say leads to confused relationships. Rather, we are thinking up what we are going to say instead of listening to them as they talk.

However, our most profound communication is deeper than words and consists of those " groanings of the spirit which cannot be uttered." Just *telling* their troubles does not necessarily make people whole. Communication must itself grow apace with the development of our capacity to love. " Even if we speak in the tongues of men and of angels, and have not this, we are as a noisy gong or a clanging cymbal." We have not matured in our love if we stop here in our growth. If many of us like this get together, we may develop a " tin-pan alley " religious cult.

Spiritual Understanding

The development of insight and understanding, knowledge, and the sense of mystery is a second type of immaturity. To the psychologically sophisticated, this sounds strange, because we tend to equate insight and maturity. But it is only a second way station in the pilgrimage to maturity. The more we try to communicate our experience as Christians, the more it is necessary for us to develop insight and understanding of ourselves and others. We learn how to be self-aware without being self-conscious and uneasy. We learn how to understand our own motivations and those of others without letting our understanding become a tool for our power to condemn ourselves and others. We learn how to be prophetic for the whole mind of God. We learn how to participate in the mysterious presence and ineffable knowledge of God without becoming a cultist or a spiritually arrogant individual.

Paul confronted persons among the Corinthians who had lost their balance on these important issues. He confronted the Greek philosophers who had " all knowledge " and often wanted it known. He also confronted the worshipers of the mystery cults of the day. He had to warn his followers of false prophets who had come among them. These persons permitted their systems of faith, organizations of knowledge, and particular " in-group " relationships to a few people to cut them off and isolate them from the larger Christian community. Apart from the power of love in interpersonal relationships, even knowledge itself becomes a divisive factor.

The reality of these truths is at every hand in the academic world of colleges and universities, seminaries, and divinity schools today. As Robert Frost says in his poem " The Cabin in the Clearing," we live " in the fond faith accumulated fact will of itself take fire and light the world up." As T. S. Eliot has aptly said:

Where is the wisdom we have lost in knowledge?
Where is the knowledge we have lost in information?
(T. S. Eliot, *Collected Poems 1909–1935;* copyright, 1936, by Harcourt, Brace and Company, Inc., and reprinted by permission.)

Likewise, analytically oriented persons are likely to stop growing at the very point of delving for more and more subtle and occult interpretations of their own motives. Having been given the power to love, they may stop at futile speculation! If we stop in the pilgrimage of our spiritual lives at this plateau, we have not moved to the highest level of maturity in building our relationships to God and others. We must move on. This is no stopping place, only a rest along the way.

THE MOVING POWER OF FAITH

A third kind of immaturity suggested by Paul is an over-dependence upon a "moving" faith, demonstrating its power. Overwhelmed by the inadequacy of our knowledge, that is, that we know in part and prophesy in part, we move upward to realize that we live by faith. We begin to "trust in the Lord with all our hearts and lean not on our own understanding." We may even tend to disparage the value of human knowledge and to decry the efforts of science. We may even discount these realities to such an extent as to set science and religion over against each other. Instead of becoming a minister of reconciliation, we may turn into an apostle of discord. Pushed by our immaturity at this point, we may feel compelled to demonstrate the power of faith, that is, that it can move mountains, help people to get well without the aid of doctors, and solve our economic distress without the necessity of work, and so on. These signs of immaturity were on hand when Paul ministered to the Corinthians, and the timelessness of his truth is obvious in that they are still to be seen in the realm of those who profess themselves to be the most powerful in faith above all others. Likewise, persons who have been in deeper analysis and psychotherapy may avoid adult decisions and impossible action by extolling the virtues of their analyst, of analysis, and of its necessity for " every living creature."

But even here in the demonstration of faith above all others, we can easily see that such " uses " of faith and therapy divide people from one another rather than nurture them in sustaining relationships of love. Paul, in another place (Gal. 5:6), says that " faith works through love." In the thirteenth chapter of First Corinthians, he tells us that he is as nothing in spiritual apprehension and maturity as long as he uses his faith as a means of gain, that is, to demonstrate his personal prowess.

THE PERIL OF ACTIVISM

A fourth type of spiritual immaturity which we encounter on our pilgrimage toward maturity is seen in our attempts to express our faith through a vocation. Here we center down on becoming proficient in our work. We become activists who are set to a task and not to be deterred from it. This is good, but it is both our hope and our destruction. Our hope is here because it means that we have a sense of responsibility that motivates us to effective action. Our destruction is here because here lies our capacity to deceive ourselves into believing that the way to relate ourselves to God is by the sheer results of our work achievements.

We burn the candle at both ends, we " rack up " our successes, we carefully record our achievements, we remind others of our most recent honors and we keep our right hand informed of what our left hand is doing at all times. Yet the inner gnawing of anxiety tells us that we are missing the main point of living and that we have gained nothing in reality. We have missed the power of the joy that comes to us by having taken the time to establish enduring and satisfying relationships to people and to inquire in the temple of the Lord how we may know and love him better. T. S. Eliot again helps us when he says:

> What life have you if you have not life together?
> There is no life that is not in community,
> And no community not lived in praise of God. . . .
> And now you live dispersed on ribbon roads,
> And no man knows or cares who is his neighbour
> Unless his neighbour makes too much disturbance,
> But all dash to and fro in motor cars,
> Familiar with the roads and settled nowhere. . . .
> And the wind shall say: "Here were decent godless people:
> Their only monument the asphalt road
> And a thousand lost golf balls."
> (From *Collected Poems 1909–1935* by T. S. Eliot, copyright, 1936, by Harcourt, Brace and Company, Inc., and reprinted with their permission.)

This is very descriptive of the person today who enters a profession and whose profession *becomes* his religion. He gives up his "body to be burned" in activistic achievement. This is his religion. He may be a doctor, a minister, a social worker, a lawyer, a psychologist, or a scientist in the physical sciences. He reaches the age of thirty-five or forty with a breathless anxiety, burned up with ambition, eaten out with tension, and fearfully apprehensive of his health. He may have the "success syndrome" of ulcers, heart pains, fatigue, confusion, and an inner sense of emptiness, meaninglessness, and boredom. He is a stranger to his family and at cross purposes with his fellow workers, and he feels that he is in a far country, far from God.

All four of these types of immaturity are really way stations along the path toward spiritual maturity in relationship to God and others. They point in the direction of maturity only when we make the supreme criterion of maturity — *agapē,* Christian love — our aim. When we reach this realization, then speaking "in the tongues of men and of angels," developing "prophetic powers" and a moving faith, achieving knowledge and insight, and giving up our bodies to be burned in activistic competition — all these appear as childish things, and at best as ways of establishing relationships of love to God and our fellow man.

THE FULL-GROWNNESS OF LOVE

Therefore, we need to arrive at an understanding of the meaning of love in terms of our maturity in relationship to God and others. In a word, without Christian love, all our other efforts at maturity thrust us into an encounter with nothingness, embroil us in futility, and make of life an empty meaninglessness that threatens our very being. We become as nothing.

Martin Buber gives a concept of interpersonal relationships in his book *I and Thou,* whereby we may think in a straight line about true maturity in relationship to God and others. He says that there are two kinds of relationships to God and others. The first relationship is the I-It relationship, in which we "use" God and others to achieve our own chosen ends, apart from a freehearted participation on the part of God and others in our choosing of the ends we would achieve. Such a relationship treats people as things and God as an occult power for our own manipulation. It is characterized by an *extractive* kind of relatedness whereby we "get out" of people what we want, develop hostile relationships to them, and then "no longer have any use for them." As we often say about people whom we do not like — or better, whom we cannot dominate, use, or manipulate — "we don't have a bit of *use* for them." Naturally, the very image of God within other persons rises up in rebellion at the tyranny of such exploitation, and a real break in interpersonal relationships occurs.

Prayer, which is the name we give to our interpersonal relationship to God, can be understood afresh from this point of view. Many persons relate themselves to God at one time or another in an I-It kind of prayer. God becomes a " purveyor to their own appetites," to use Browning's phrase, one who caters to their own chosen ends in life, ends that have been chosen without consulting or considering his creative plan for life. A fervent desire to achieve some chosen end becomes, for all practical purposes, a god, an idol, and the eternal God and Father of our Lord Jesus Christ becomes the servant of the idol — in our own deluded way of thinking, to say the least. As such, prayer becomes a type of magic, that is, the management of infinite powers by finite persons. This is particularly true in the search for health and financial success.

Buber suggests a second kind of relationship that is radically different from the I-It relationship. He calls it the I-Thou relationship. Here we relate ourselves to God and to one another as *persons,* and not as things. Persons are ends within themselves rather than means to ulterior ends. The content of the Christian meaning of love can be put into Buber's concept of the I-Thou relationship, thereby aiding in a vital discovery of the meaning of the prophetic conception of love that had its roots in Hebrew thinking. Love is the capacity to accept responsibility for others and to relate to them in terms of their essential rather than their instrumental value. People are more than sheep or cattle; they are more than mere measuring sticks for our own ego achievements; they are more than tools for us to exploit; they are essentially valuable in and of themselves as " persons for whom Christ died," as having been initially made in "the image of God."

Likewise, God is the chief end of our existence, not we the chief end of his being. We find our prayers filled with all the fullness of God when we glorify him rather than attempt to subvert him to our petty pursuits in life. Prayer becomes adoration, thanksgiving, participation in fellowship, and the transformation of our selfhood into the likeness of him more than mere petition and a childish whining after one toy of desire and another. These things are added unto us, not as the end intention, but as the "afterthought by-product" of God's already existing knowledge of our needs.

The practical outworking of such a relationship of mature love of God and others is obvious in the thinking of Paul.

We become more secure and can be freed more and more of our impatience and unkindness toward others. We can evaluate their misunderstandings of us in a new light: the light of our failure to communicate our real motives clearly and in the light of our "inhuman use of them as humans." We are not so watchful of self-comparisons, because our own status is built by their success. The necessity for arrogance and rudeness is nil in genuinely secure people who feel that they have been accepted and understood for what they are really worth: persons for whom Christ died. Such persons value one another so highly that there is no need that they build one another or themselves up through bragging and boasting. They can only rejoice in the success of others and be grieved by others' failures. The relationships of life become more enduring, and they "last on."

In the relationships of love, Jesus Christ is always breaking through in some new revelation of his love through persons' concern for one another. Mature Christians are always searching their relationships to others and testing their knowledge of God with others. They live in the constant hope that God will again make himself known to them in their breaking of bread with one another. Their speaking, their prophecy, their understanding, and their faith and works are all set into a new contextual meaning of the love of God. This love, made known to them in the abiding relationship of Christ to them in the new covenant of his blood, becomes their clear channel of interpersonal relationship to one another.

6

SUFFERING AND SELF-DEFENSE

So Joseph went after his brothers, and found them at Dothan. They saw him afar off, and before he came near to them they conspired against him to kill him. They said to one another, "Here comes this dreamer. Come now, let us kill him and throw him into one of the pits; then we shall say that a wild beast has devoured him, and we shall see what will become of his dreams." But when Reuben heard it, he delivered him out of their hands, saying, "Let us not take his life." And Reuben said to them, "Shed no blood; cast him into this pit here in the wilderness, but lay no hand upon him" — that he might rescue him out of their hand, to restore him to his father. So when Joseph came to his brothers, they stripped him of his robe, the long robe with sleeves that he wore; and they took him and cast him into a pit. The pit was empty, there was no water in it.

— Gen. 37:17-24.

JOSEPH hit the bottom of the pit, and it grounded him to a bruised halt. He clenched his teeth as he recovered from his fall. They struck the mouthful of grit he had caught in falling. He searched the bottom of the pit for some water, but "the pit was empty, there was no water in it." It was as empty as the feeling in his stomach. With his own hands, then, he cleansed his mouth; for his own wounds, only his own dirty hands, were a comfort. Gone were the pampering hands of his parents. Gone were the soft protections of a life at the side of his fond, elderly father. Gone were the dreamy pretensions of ruling over his whole family. Gone were the filmy fantasies that his brothers would be pleased with his success and his childlike achievements. He had learned the hard way that they did not love him for his dreams of dominion and his grandiose patterns for success. What a jolt!

Out of the Depths

Only our imagination can guide us as we try to determine what Joseph thought in the depths of the pit into which he had been cast. Did he feel himself hopelessly lost and without possibility of even life itself in the pit of despair that was his? He must have felt the inner resignation that comes from seeing absolutely no way out of an unalterable situation. He felt the clutch of forces over which he had not one vestige of control. He sensed the despair of being totally helpless. Such absolute resignation brought him a feeling of being entirely dependent upon the grace of God.

The reality of God, which had hitherto been obscured to him by his own dreams of ruling the world, now became " a very present help in time of trouble." Joseph's defenses against his real humanity, his real helplessness, were for the first time in his life at rest. He had lost everything, up to the hilt of losing life itself. Only life itself remained. Only life itself mattered. He no longer had to pretend, to impress, to cajole, to maneuver, to brag, to boss, in order to exist. With a strange sense of freedom from himself, from dependence upon his brothers' opinions of him, from his father's pampering, and from his restless striving, Joseph probably for the first time slept a dreamless sleep. He had found out what his own dreams meant, and they were no longer necessary to his existence. The defense rested.

~

On awakening, a new light broke over Joseph. It bolted into his awareness as a question. Why did Reuben say: " Let us not take his life. . . . Shed no blood; cast him into this pit here in the wilderness, but lay no hand upon him "? Could this be the redemptive love of the God about whom he had heard his father talk? Could it be that this terrible thing which had come to pass was thought by his brothers to be evil against him, but that God was meaning it to be good? As Joseph reflected on the meaning of this shift of intention coming from within Reuben, he heard the chatter of strange voices far up above near the rim of the pit. Above the commotion he could hear the voice of Judah: " Let us sell him to the Ishmaelites. What profit is it if we slay our brother and conceal his blood? "

A man has to be on bottom before even bad news sounds good. At any other time in his life the threat to sell him into slavery would have been evil in itself, but that which his brothers intended to be evil for him sounded to him as God's intention to redeem him. Then a great quietness came over the crowd. A life line came slithering down the side of the pit to draw Joseph up out of it. And his brothers sold him to the Ishmaelites for twenty pieces of silver.

From our comfortable point of view, to be sold into bondage as a slave would be as bad as death; but from the point of view of Joseph on the bottom of the pit, death was not a matter of speculation but an immediate possibility. Therefore, slavery was the redeeming hand of God himself. Joseph went, bound, with the slave traders. He mused on the way in which God had used the mercenary intention of Judah to save him and to prepare him, Joseph, as an instrument tempered in fire, for the destiny ahead of him. He could say:

I waited patiently for the Lord;
  he inclined to me and heard my cry.
He drew me up from the desolate pit,
  out of the miry bog,
and set my feet upon a rock,
  making my steps secure.
He put a new song in my mouth,
  a song of praise to our God.
Many will see and fear,
  and put their trust in the Lord.
                    — Ps. 40:1-3.

THE CHANGING POWER OF FAILURE

Vital changes in our way of life do not take place as long
as we can " succeed " in our own eyes by the way of life
we have. Until we " as we are " have been deeply threatened,
we do not tend to try to become other than what we are. In
fact, at this point it can be rightly said that some people's
lives have to go from bad to worse before they begin to
get better. This is not always true, but it is true often enough
to expect this to happen in our own situations. In this sense,
trouble is like fever in the body: it indicates the need for
radical and immediate change. Such was the case of Joseph.
By all outward standards he was a " success," so much so
that his brethren envied him. But the way of life whereby
he had become successful desperately needed changing.

Joseph had been living defensively, always making a case
for him before his brothers, compensating for his youth
with brilliance, compensating for his tardy birth by dream-
ing dreams of his greatness, and offsetting his brethren's
seniority with favors from his father. This accents a basic
law of life: a defensive life tends to crumble under a test
and a person is thrust into despair, even as was Joseph. Defensive living inevitably tangles a person in one set of unhappy relationships after another. As long as one feels that

he has to "make a case" for himself and "justify" his own right to breathe, he defeats himself with his defenses. When the clutch of circumstance closes in upon him, he may "leave off," or, as the lawyers say, "let the case rest," rather than talk wordily on to confusion. If he can let the "defense rest," he suddenly discovers a kind of security he has never known before and God has a chance to begin working in his life. When the defense rests, the providential work of God has just begun. Man's extremity is God's opening. Not only Joseph's experience, but also the experience of other witnesses in a variety of situations, attests to the truth of this working hypothesis of living.

The Act of Surrender

Life is filled with unalterable situations. Persons are clutched by habits and forces over which they seem not to have one vestige of control. Persons find themselves exhausted, helpless, and stymied in their attempts at solving a veritable maze of difficulties that, they discover, in reality has no exit. They encounter futility and meaninglessness, helplessness, and defeat. They suddenly surrender the whole feverish effort and land on the bottom of despair. In this act of surrender, however, an almost miraculous change tends to occur if the person is not tempted by false solutions, and if he sees himself as he really is in the process. In this act of surrender itself, a person is made whole again through the activating power of God, because to experience total helplessness and to feel the utter sense of being in God's mercy is the beginning of salvation.

For example, Fyodor Dostoevsky was condemned to death by the firing squad. He had no way out of the death sentence. Just as he was to be killed — the soldiers with their guns loaded, shouldered, and cocked to fire — the emperor issued a reprieve. Dostoevsky, later commenting in his book *The Idiot,* says: "What if I were not to die! What if I could go back to life — what eternity! And it would all be mine! I would turn every minute into an age; I would lose nothing, I would count every minute as it passed, I would not waste one! " (*The Idiot,* tr. by Constance Garnett, p. 55. Modern Library, Inc., 1935.) When the reprieve came, it was as if he had actually died and was living a resurrected existence.

A close friend tells of his experience of horror and despair in the fiercest fighting of the Battle for Europe in World War II. He and his men had been on an expedition into Holland, and all but a handful had been killed. They returned to a rest area and sat down together. He spoke to them, saying: "It is as if we had been born again back out of death itself, and life can never be the same again. It seems as if I were as Lazarus, called back from death to live a life of redemptive witness among people who are yet to face such desperation."

Another example: Dr. Harry M. Tiebout wrote a scholarly article in the *Quarterly Journal of Alchohol Studies* that was reprinted in *Pastoral Psychology* (March, 1950). He called this article "The Act of Surrender in the Treatment of the Alcoholic." The act of surrender is described as the resting of defenses toward life and the adoption of a teachable openness to reality. He says that the act of surrender comes about when "the forces of defiance and grandiosity actually cease to function effectively." (Whereas Joseph had not been bothered with alcohol, this is nevertheless exactly what happened to him. The forces of defiance and grandiosity ceased to function effectively.) Dr. Tiebout says that when this happens, an "individual is wide open to life: he can listen and learn without conflict and fighting back. . . . In other words, an act of surrender is an occasion when the individual no longer fights life but accepts it."

One of Dr. Tiebout's patients, an alcoholic, tells about this actually happening to him in an AA meeting:

> I was licked. I'd tried everything and nothing had worked. My wife was packing to leave me; my job was going to blow up in my face. I was desperate when I went to my first meeting of the AA. When I got there, something happened. I don't know to this day (a year later) what it was, but I took a look at the men and women there and I knew they had something I needed; so I said to myself: "I'll listen to what they have to tell me." From that time on, things have been different.
> *(Ibid.)*

When he hit the bottom of his pit of despair, suddenly the worst turned the best to the brave, as Browning has said, and things began not only to look, but to be, different.

Occasionally one meets business and professional men and women who consider their work as a fight for existence. As one salesman told me in a store once, " If you make a living today, sir, you've got to fight and fight and fight." And one preacher described his ministerial existence from the pulpit, " Life is a hard battle with a short stick." Even Moses, in his work, " wore himself and the people out," according to his father-in-law, Jethro, in his feeling that the whole job had to be done by him and him alone. Life gets old for the highly competitive and restlessly struggling worker, and work itself becomes a sort of addiction for him. Illness, active professional opposition, staleness, stagnation of spirit, or any of a host of other destroying contenders may thrust such a person into a pit of despair in which he is forced to cease to fight for his place in the world and to accept the limitations in his ability to do everything. This calls for a sort of surrender, a " giving up," a thrusting of oneself upon the simplicities of life, for life itself is in peril. Men and women who have had their first phase of success in life undergo this in the late thirties and early forties. As one man, in the heat of a crisis of the kind I am describing here, put it:

> And they said to me, " Go to, now — let us have a fight."
> And I said to them, " But what are we fighting about and what are we fighting for? "
> And they said to me, " Oh we are fighting about first one thing and then the other."
> And I said, " But what are we fighting for? "
> And I heard only a buzzing among them. A few giggles punctured the buzzing.
> So — I went away and climbed a great high hill and looked at the blinking neon signs across a great wide river on which hovered the commerce of nations.
> Then I heard the Lord say: " Do you want to know what the fighting is for? I will tell you: Two yards of sackcloth, a bucket of ashes, and a quart of gall. The sackcloth and ashes will be to those who still can feel enough after the fight to sense its futility and repent. The quart of gall will be for those who can no longer feel either for themselves or for others and can taste only that which is bitter."

The Unmerited Grace of God

Jesus and Paul gave us the distinctly religious dimension of this experience which has its roots in the nature of human personality. Essentially the problem with Joseph and with our contemporaries who live defensively is that he and they felt, feel, and will always feel (until they are thrown into a pit) that they must earn the right to believe, the favor of the Heavenly Father, and a place in the world by their own unaided efforts. They know not a faith in God that rests without defense upon the fact that he has bought us with a price and we do not have to buy him with a price. It is not he who needs us, but we who need him. As the psalmist interprets the mind of God:

> Hear, O my people, and I will speak,
>   O Israel, I will testify against you.
>   I am God, your God. . . .
> For every beast of the forest is mine,
>   the cattle on a thousand hills. . . .
> If I were hungry, I would not tell you;
>   for the world and all that is in it is mine. . . .
> And call upon me in the day of trouble;
>   I will deliver you, and you shall glorify me.
>   — Ps. 50:7, 10, 12, 15.

The moment a person takes the attitude that he *must* earn the favor of God, he moves upon the assumption that he *can* earn that favor. He is only one step from assuming that he is more powerful than God and can manipulate him. Therefore, he is alone in his struggle to save himself; this drives him deeper and deeper into effort, closer and closer to his own helplessness and to the loneliness of his own despair.

But on the other hand, when he strikes bottom and his defenses actually rest, he becomes open to his own frailty and accepts his own humanity. If he is so compulsive that he cannot see this for himself, his brothers will react to him with such hostility that a pit of circumstances finally closes about him. In other words, if his own inner insight and prayerful relationship to God do not convince him of his true situation, the aggression of his brothers toward his defensive way of life will thrust him into a pit of their choosing. If their opposition fails, then only a miracle when he is all alone can save him. For instance, Jacob was alone on the River Jabbok and wrestled with God who changed him from one who had " supplanted " to one who had " striven " with God himself, and gave him a reminder of his weakness.

The lively word of hope in the Christian gospel speaks clearly to us. However, we can profit by the experience of other people and experience the pit of despair vicariously to such an extent that we are delivered without the damage associated with alcoholism, without the hideous ostracism of our brothers, and without blundering along our way. We can enter the depths of the feelings of others and draw upon the strength of their experience. In fact, the heart of the Christian gospel is this: In a unique way never enacted before or since, the Lord Jesus Christ *voluntarily* " descended into the pit of our own making" and suffered in our behalf. He " descended into hell," the creed says. He took upon himself not only the pit but also bondage and redemption in our behalf. Now we can be crucified with him, we can be buried with him, and through his grace we can be raised to walk with him in the newness of life. This is his way of saying to us that while we are yet sinners, he accepts us and affirms his love for us and causes his experience of deliverance from the grave to bring about our redemption.

STANDING ALONE BEFORE GOD

Such was the appearance of the likeness of the glory of the Lord. And when I saw it, I fell upon my face, and I heard the voice of one speaking. And he said to me, " Son of man, stand upon your feet, and I will speak with you." And when he spoke to me, the Spirit entered into me and set me upon my feet; and I heard him speaking to me.

—Ezek. 1:28 to 2:1-2.

Stand therefore, having girded your loins with truth, and having put on the breastplate of righteousness, and having shod your feet with the equipment of the gospel of peace; above all taking the shield of faith, with which you can quench all the flaming darts of the evil one. And take the helmet of salvation, and the sword of the Spirit, which is the word of God.

—Eph. 6:14-17.

WE AS human beings, through the unfolding drama of our creation, redemption, and preservation by God, have been made to stand erect. This is another one of our distinctives as persons. Some of the developmental psychologists have heavily emphasized the importance of weaning, training in cleanliness, and the like, in the achievement of emotional stability in a growing child. But not enough of them have appreciated the profound meaning that learning to stand alone and to walk on his own two feet has for a child. Here he or she is no longer forced to lie supinely in the parents' arms, nor, at best, be confined to the narrow limits of crawling on all fours. As if overnight, when a child learns to stand and walk, he undergoes a transformation, as any mother who has chased a toddler can attest! Exploring, questing, peering into, pulling out the kitchen utensils and the contents of the closets and dresser drawers, he is on a pilgrimage that only sleep and death will interrupt or end. About the same time, he has learned to talk. The new-found independence of walking is coupled with the joy of communication with his parents. The threat of " talking back " to his parents is mixed by the alchemy of love with the promise of fellowship and communion with the child.

These leaves taken from the notebooks of the growth of a human child are prototypical and symbolic of man's relationship with God, the Heavenly Father. The eternal God humbled Ezekiel in a transforming vision. He taught him to stand on his feet, and challenged him to commune with him. Then he commissioned him to be a prophet. The letter to the Ephesians tells us to " put on the whole armor of God, . . . and having done all, to stand," and to commune with God at all times in prayer.

The Sovereignty of God

The overarching sovereignty and majesty of God strike the reader of both passages of Scripture to which reference has just been made. The " likeness of the glory of the Lord " in his total otherness and drastic difference from man swept Ezekiel up into a beatific vision. This vision strained the limits of human language for description. Its overpowering magnificence thrust Ezekiel to the ground, and he fell upon his face. He was filled with the fear and trembling like the holy dread that felled the apostle Paul on the road to Damascus. For, as Sören Kierkegaard has said, when we stand alone before God, we are filled with fear and trembling. This anxiety is inevitable as we encounter God face to face.

Yet, a man is anxious and torn asunder in all other relationships until he has both met and been met by God in such event in eternity. Until this time, he is an idolater of all lesser authorities. He clutches at first one and then another tower of strength for security. He clutches first at the strength of his parents as though they were gods. Then he lays hold of his nearest friend as though that friend could provide him with lasting security. Then he shifts to a member of the opposite sex and makes a divinity of that one. Later he may become what William H. Whyte, Jr., has called an " organization man " and make his social class, his union, his profession, his lodge, his church, his denomination, or the like, into an escape from the anxiety, the suffering, and the distress of personal confrontation with God as the sovereign of his life.

We may be thrust flat on our faces as was true of Ezekiel, or flat on our backs, as is true of many a sick person, or driven by our own self-deification until our backs are " against the wall " in desperation. In any event, God remains a hidden God and does not really become a revealed God to us until we are, by some such clutching circumstance, made acutely aware of our own humanity as over against his infinite sovereignty. Then we are on the verge of his revelation of himself to us. Before we can lay hold of the power to stand before God, our own surreptitious and sneaky feeling that we ourselves are God must be shaken loose. As the letter to the Hebrews puts it, we must have removed " what is shaken, . . . in order that what cannot be shaken may remain. Therefore let us be grateful for receiving a kingdom that cannot be shaken, and thus let us offer to

God acceptable worship, with reverence and awe; for our God is a consuming fire." In other words, the humility of dependence upon and subjection to the eternal God necessarily precedes the privilege of standing before and talking with God. This is the brunt of the message of reconciliation in Jesus Christ. He humbled himself, took upon himself the form of a servant, and found himself fashioned in the likeness of mankind. Therefore, God exalted him and gave to him a name that is above every other name. As Jesus himself puts it, " every one who exalts himself will be humbled, and he who humbles himself will be exalted."

THE DIGNITY OF MAN

However, the truth of Jesus' paradox is roundly questioned today by those who see no place for the authority of a sovereign God. Some contemporary psychologists have rejected the classical Calvinistic statement of the sovereignty of God on the grounds that it disparages and desecrates the dignity of human personality. We are told that only a humanistic kind of religion that rejects the so-called authoritarianism of the revelation of a sovereign God really contributes to the upbuilding of human personality. We must grant them that the authoritarianism of totalitarian religious leaders has repeatedly latched on to the doctrine of the sovereignty of God to justify their own needs for power.

Nevertheless, when we probe more deeply into the Biblical understanding of the Holy One of Israel as the prophets and Jesus knew and related themselves to him, we have solid reason to challenge both the shallow understanding of the sovereignty of God on the part of the psychologists and the nefarious misuse of the doctrine of the sovereignty of God by ecclesiastical power politics. The eternal God, seeing Ezekiel prostrate before him, commanded him to " stand upon his feet." This was no relationship of servility, benevolent paternalism, or self-erasure. God, to the contrary, challenged Ezekiel to selfhood in responsible relationship between the creature and his creator. This was God's affirmation of his own image in Ezekiel. For the sacredness of human personality is rooted and grounded in the character of God as our creator. This sacredness derives both its meaning and its direction from the Personhood of God.

In the missionary enterprise set in motion by William Carey, vivid examples of this principle can be found. For instance, Carey, instead of superimposing British culture upon the Indians, subjected himself to the disciplines of learning the ways of India. As S. Pearce Carey, in his biography of William Carey, says, " Carey became India in order that India might become Christian." He and many missionaries after him, in bringing first themselves and then the natives into subjection to the claims of God in Christ, opened the way whereby the natives discovered their true selfhood as Indians. Frank Laubach, in evaluating Christian missions in the Orient, said that the present crisis of the upsurging self-consciousness of the Oriental people indirectly is a result of Christian missionaries' message of the dignity of a person in Christ. This message actually got across. They were convinced that they really were persons, and not just the " nobodies " of the earth. Now he challenges Western culture to make room for the new and emerging self-respect wrought in the Orient by Christian missions of the past hundred years. They are learning to " stand on their feet."

The same thing can be said of the Negro, the Indian, the Japanese, and the Mexican in this country. We cannot, in the vanity of " being nice " and " free of prejudice," insist that these persons become " anglicized " to such an extent that the world will be deprived of the unique contribution that they have to make *as* Negroes, *as* Indians, *as* Japanese, and *as* Mexicans. As long as the thrust of their desire for freedom causes them to grovel in the dust of disrespect for their own race, they can never achieve the dignity that " standing on their own before God " can afford them. Therefore, in our efforts to " integrate " them, we shall actually annihilate them as a people if we do not expect them to stand up on their own feet as a race and respect their own separate and individual identity as a race under God. Until a race achieves a selfhood of its own, community with others is absorption, not fellowship. Otherwise, our sense of guilt and their sense of inferiority will conspire to stalemate our most exuberant enthusiasm for " brotherhood." No enduring " brotherhood " is possible apart from the sovereignty of God which supplies the ground of all genuine self-respect, dignity of man, and fellowship among men.

The Invitation to Communion

The recognition of the sovereignty of God is a prelude to becoming a self before God, to " standing upon our feet " as a person in his presence. Being a self in our own right, having a sense of integrity and personhood in relationship to God, in turn, is the prelude to spiritual communion with God. Such are the primary conditions of prayer. The Pharisee prayed " within himself " and had no real communion with God as he thanked God that he was not as other men. The Lord heard and justified the publican who considered himself a sinner. He caused him to stand upon his feet in order that he, the Lord, might speak with him. He lifted Ezekiel out of his contrition into the fellowship of face-to-face communion, creating a relationship of prayer.

The sense of guilt and personal unworthiness is the main

barrier to effective communion with God. The gnawing sense of inferiority or the overweening sense of superiority in either instance annihilates the communion of man with God, insulates the experience of prayer, and negates the fellowship of the Spirit of God. To the contrary, when the Spirit of God enters us, he enables us to stand before God in prayer. We can, with boldness, because of the sacrifice of the Lord Jesus Christ and the intercession of the Holy Spirit, make our confessions, petitions, and inquiries known unto the Heavenly Father. This comradeship of prayer, upon the initiative and invitation of God, is the antithesis of the subjugation of personality. This is the adornment and fruition of man's highest potential. In prayer the God-shaped vacuum of man's loneliness, even in the most intimate of human relationships, is overcome by the conversation with God. The essential question of religion is not whether or not God exists, for as many proofs one way as the other can be academically posed against each other. The essential question of religion is whether or not God and man, granted that both exist, can genuinely commune with each other. The heart of the Christian revelation is that God has taken the initiative and through his Spirit enabled man to stand in his presence through the forgiveness of sins in Christ. In Christ we have access to God, and can commune with him as a colaborer. He is our God and we are his people. In Christian prayer, therefore, we do not find a groveling picture of human personality. We find God commanding us to stand upon our feet in order that he may speak with us.

The Glory of God in the Christian Calling

The fellowship of prayer as Ezekiel experienced it resulted in a clear-cut sense of mission and calling. The like-

ness of the glory of God took its plainest and clearest form
in the commission he gave to Ezekiel. He fell in humility
before God. The Spirit of God entered him and caused
him to stand upon his feet. He communed with God. As he
communed with God, he received the commission of God:
" Son of man, I send you to the people of Israel . . . and
whether they hear or refuse to hear . . . they will know
that there has been a prophet among them." Ezekiel's ministry would not be conditioned by the " other-directedness "
of the approval or disapproval of the people. The clarity of
his mission as a prophet of God would be apparent, even
to those who rejected the claims of his message. He received,
by reason of his face-to-face relationship with God, an au-
thentic, unmistakable identity all his own. Both his friends
and his enemies would know him as a prophet of God
among men.

This clarity of purpose also shines transparently through
the steady resolve that embues the Ephesian correspondence
of the New Testament. W. O. Carver sees " the glory of
God in the Christian calling " as the controlling theme of
the letter to the Ephesians. All the way through the letter
(it is especially apparent in the section chosen as a text for
this sermon) the resolute and courageous sense of clear
direction under God fills every paragraph. The Christian
man is pulled up out of his cringing fearfulness and told
to " put on the whole armor of God," to " stand against the
wiles of the devil." The command to strongness in the
strength of the Lord's might is quickly followed by a command to " pray at all times in the Spirit."

The sovereign grace and glory of God lays hold of man
and brings him to the fullness of the stature of his sonship
in Christ. But this fulfillment of man's personality is not for
the self-centered enhancement of man's personal vanity. God

shapes man for a commission and a calling, even in the darkest hours of his suffering. He gives him a vocation, a calling, and a commission, and, as John Knox said, gives him mortal life until his work is done. From this comes the dignity of man under the sovereignty of God.

SUFFERING AND
THE SENSE OF DIRECTION

By faith Abraham obeyed when he was called to go out to
a place which he was to receive as an inheritance; and he went
out, not knowing where he was to go. By faith he sojourned
in the land of promise, as in a foreign land, living in tents with
Isaac and Jacob, heirs with him of the same promise. For he
looked forward to the city which has foundations, whose
builder and maker is God. . . .

These all died in faith, not having received what was prom-
ised, but having seen it and greeted it from afar, and having
acknowledged that they were strangers and exiles on the
earth. . . . Therefore, God is not ashamed to be called their
God, for he has prepared for them a city. . . . So Jesus also
suffered outside the gate in order to sanctify the people through
his own blood. Therefore let us go forth to him outside the
camp, bearing abuse for him. For here we have no lasting city,
but we seek the city which is to come.

— Heb. 11:8-10, 13, 16; 13:12-14.

POLLY ADLER, a little Jewish girl, was sent alone early in
this century to this country when she was but twelve
years of age. She lived with distant relatives and then with
first one stranger and then another who would take her in.
She struggled desperately for survival in the garment dis-
tricts of New York City, far from her family and home in
Poland. She was trapped in the hectic existence of the
prostitution rackets of New York City and became a pro-
curess in this sordid business. As a woman, she lived her

life in the midst of tragedy, gross sin, and sheer calamity of existence. But she came to a dramatic reversal of direction in her life and said:

> And suddenly it seemed to me that there was no direction to my life at all. I had been rocking back and forth for years over the same waters, running before the storm in bad weather and hoving to when it was calm. Yes, I had been wrecked and in dry dock and refitted. I had even learned the compass and a star or two, but I was just keeping afloat; I wasn't going anywhere. (Polly Adler in *A House Is Not a Home,* p. 273. Popular Library, 1953.)

The plight of Polly Adler is the suffering of many persons who turn to pastors, doctors, business people, and other counselors for guidance. They can accurately say: " I am just beating around from one thing to another." " I don't know where I am going." " Every day is like the one before; I just don't seem to be anywhere else than I was the day before." " Where is it all going to lead to? " These questions are the bubbling up of the deep need of every human being to have a clear sense of direction. Lewis Sherrill has aptly said that, for some people, life is a treadmill that is only one step removed from life as a merry-go-round. Neither is going anywhere in particular. Sherrill also said that for other people life is a saga, or a battle. They perish unless they have something to fight. But for other people, Sherrill says, life is a pilgrimage. This pilgrimage requires a clear sense of direction. Therefore, when people ask where they are going, they are essentially asking the question of the basic meaning of life. When they start answering this question, they find that the source to which they most often turn for a sense of direction determines the kind of person one becomes, the character of one's being. In fact, persons are to be distinguished from one another, not by the color of their skin, the social class from which they come, or the particular creed that they espouse. Men and women are known by that which they love, the source to which they turn for the main directions of their lives. As Augustine has said, "the City of God is known by what it loves."

David Riesman, in *The Lonely Crowd,* has penetratingly analyzed the character of American people today in terms of the main sources of their sense of direction. He says that there are three major types of people. To his three types I would like to add a fourth type of person in terms of the basic sense of direction that guides him. There is, according to Reisman, the tradition-directed person, the inner-directed person, the other-directed person. The fourth, which I am adding, is the faith-directed person.

THE TRADITION-DIRECTED PERSON

The tradition-directed person charts the course of his life by the road map of the experience of other people who have gone before him. His culture, his family, his forebears, his church, as they live in tradition, become his main source of direction in every sphere of life. When asked if a thing should be done, he always inquires, "Was it done before and how did they do it?" He has the remarkable capacity to profit by the experience of others. If he goes to college, it may well be because of the tradition of his family, the solid culture in which those who carry his name simply "always do this." For him, religion is a heritage. Like a brilliant young Jewish student of mine, he may say, as she said, "We Jews have a heritage to nourish, to cherish, and to maintain!"

Yet this person's sense of direction is already drawn for him and he is related to it passively and permanently. The road map of his tradition is drawn, catalogued, and set before him by others. He may well be in the position in which the tradition tells us that Paul found Timothy. The older preacher reminded the younger one that the faith of the Lord Jesus Christ dwelt first in his grandmother Lois and in his mother, Eunice. Timothy had a rich tradition. Yet, he was reminded that he himself must rekindle the gift of God that was within him. He must thrust aside any spirit of timidity in behalf of the personally activated spirit of power, love, and self-control. In this event the tradition is no longer just a tradition. It has become personal. The road map has become a part of the traveler himself. It has been committed to memory and has become second nature. Then the person begins to look beyond his tradition for his sense of direction. He is borne out of tradition into a selfhood of his own. This leads us to the second type of person in terms of sense of direction, namely, the inner-directed, or self-directed, person.

THE INNER-DIRECTED PERSON

The inner-directed person has transcended the dead letter of tradition. He may well have an abiding tradition as a sense of direction, but it has become so much a part of him that it works internally rather than externally. He has given his inward affirmation and personal volition to the tradition in such a way that it is a part of his true selfhood. But more than this he has become an individual in his own right. He has achieved a personal sense of identity. He has, as C. G. Jung says, " come up out of the fog bank of the crowd and discovered his own inner uniqueness." Henceforth he gets his direction from his internal image of himself as an individual. He judges where he is going and what he is doing by his inner conviction of who he is. This is not just a self-centeredness. It is a clear awareness of one's own uniqueness, individuality, and personal calling in life.

You, as a person in your own right, master your tradition rather than allow yourself to be mastered by your tradition. Instead of depending upon the road maps of tradition to tell you what to do, your clear conception of yourself as a person in your own right has become a sort of inner gyroscope that guides you. Like a ship's compass, it keeps your life on its course after you have once been headed in the right direction. This gyroscopic guide, your inner selfhood, becomes a compass that is not affected by magnetism or external movements of others.

We have an amazing lack of this kind of directedness in our world today. We are called to live our lives in an atmosphere of broken and shattered traditions. We are like the priest in Alan Paton's *Cry, the Beloved Country,* who said that the counselors of South Africa have counsel for everything except the matter of the broken traditions of their people. We live in an era of spiritual confusion as we make the toilsome and bloody transition from one sure tradition to a new grasp of a worthy tradition that is not yet clear to us. Robert Frost, in his poem " The Cabin in the Clearing " (printed in *The New York Times Book Review,* February 3, 1952), vividly describes the fogginess of the average American as to his personal identity and clarity of selfhood. He imagines a conversation between the smoke from the cabin in the clearing and the damp mist that gathers in the early morning around the cabin. The mist says to the smoke:

> I don't believe the sleepers in this house know where they are . . . and still I doubt if they know where they are. And I begin to fear they never will.

Then the smoke responds with a sage kind of wisdom, saying:

If the day ever comes when they know who
They are they may know better where they are.
But who they are is too much to believe —
Either for them or the onlooking world.

The Christian faith, as reflected in the New Testament, lays heavy emphasis on the imperative that one be born again, that he become a son of God, that through faith in the Lord Jesus Christ he may discover a new being, a new sense of identity, a clear awareness of who he is. Christians can remember the time when they were " separated from Christ, alienated from the commonwealth of Israel, and strangers to the covenants of promise, having no hope and without God in the world " (Eph. 2:12). But through the reconciling power of Jesus Christ they can say now that they are " no longer strangers and sojourners, but . . . fellow citizens with the saints and members of the household of God, built upon the foundation of the apostles and prophets, Christ Jesus himself being the chief cornerstone . . ." (Eph. 2:19-20). The writer of First Peter says that whereas they had been " no people," now they were the people of God. They had achieved a clear sense of identity, a given sense of personhood. This was who they were. They were Christians.

The mist and smoke clear away from our sense of direction, and we begin to feel ourselves a child of destiny when this birth of a new life takes place. This identity then becomes the basis of our moral choices, the inner source of our spiritual direction. We do not do things and we do do things, not because someone else said so, but because they either are or are not keeping with our sense of personhood in Christ, our self-chosen sense of destiny and mission that to us is a calling. We do not, as Phillips translates Romans 12:2, " let the world around us squeeze us into its own mould." Rather, we let God " remould our minds from within."

However, the quicksands of individualism and the temptations of self-centeredness are readily at hand for the Christian pilgrim who has arrived at this sense of identity. He is tempted, even as the Son of God was tempted in the wilderness, to dissociate himself from his fellow human beings, and thus to arrogate to himself a position above them. His inner-direction becomes self-idolatry. Thomas Wolfe, for instance, could accurately say that his whole effort for years was " to fathom his own design, to explore his own channels, and to discover his own ways." He could, with unswerving devotion, integrity, and purity of purpose, recount this vision of his life and not let it be " menaced, altered, or weakened by anyone." He could lash out at his editor and say, " Don't take the Pacific Limited and switch it down the siding toward Hogwart Junction." However, he lived his life in isolation, loneliness, and self-gratification. He rejected quite roundly the claims of any community upon him.

In the distinctly Christian understanding of inner individuality and personal freedom, this is always set within the context of responsible love for and commitment to " the household of God." Therefore, this leads to the third source of direction for our lives, namely, the community of others with whom we live.

The Other-directed Person

A third source of direction upon which we call is the community to which we belong. This is composed of the organizations to which we belong, the social groups whose approval we value most, and the crowd with whom we are most predominantly competing. Riesman calls this kind of spiritual direction " other-directedness."

The apostle Paul, in dealing with the highly individualized vagaries of the spiritual life that were rife among the Corinthians, reminded them of the spiritual gift of community within them as one of the guides for checking their inner sense of direction. The household of God provided the context for the ongoing pilgrimage of the individual, and his personal pilgrimage could never be dissociated from responsible relationship to the ongoing "people of God." Even in the high exaltation of the book of Hebrews, we find that the race that the Christian is running is in the arena of a "great cloud of witnesses" who are gathered about watching the contest. From the fellowship of the saints we draw inspiration for achieving the destiny that God has set before us as individuals. The presence or absence of this inspiration often makes the difference between arrival at the destination that we ourselves under God have chosen.

But Reisman is right when he points out that this too may become an idolatry. He deplores Americans' "other-directedness" as, in the absence of old-time road maps or tradition and with the lack of an inner sense of spiritual self-direction, they anxiously consult the radar of public opinion before making any decision. They are like the shepherd of Gyges, of whom Plato spoke, who, when he discovered a magic ring that made him undetectable by other people, regardless of what he did, became the most immoral man in all his country because he no longer had the directing power of public opinion. We are worshipers of what Francis Bacon called the "idols of the market place." Whatever brings the highest price on the market of public opinion determines the course of our action. William H. Whyte, Jr., in his book *The Organization Man,* has almost cynically described the way in which the inner directions of spiritual individuality are snuffed out by the desperate needs of Americans to belong to a group, a type, a union, a uniform sales organization, a political or social or religious pressure group of conformity. He says:

> Where the immersion of the individual used to be cause for grumbling and a feeling of independence lost, the organization man of today is now welcoming it. He is not attempting to reverse the trend and to cut down the deference paid to the group; he is working to increase it, and . . . he is erecting what is almost a secular religion. (William H. Whyte, Jr., *The Organization Man,* p. 52. Doubleday & Company, Inc., 1957.)

These are times in which it is difficult to steer the course between the Scylla of hyperindividualism and the Charybdis of the organization man of whom Whyte speaks. But this is a tension that we must in faith take upon ourselves. Apart from an active faith in a living God, we cannot bear this burden alone. Therefore, we must with a probing sense of necessity dig for a deeper and more dependable source of direction than we have yet found in our spiritual exploration.

THE FAITH-DIRECTED PERSON

The writer of the book of Hebrews adds a new dimension to our sense of direction if we take him seriously. He gives full appreciation to the role of tradition in our sense of direction. He lays full emphasis on the importance of a strong sense of personal identity as a means of direction. He leaves us with a vivid consciousness of the importance of a vital community about us as a guiding and encouraging source of direction. But he puts at the center of all of these a living faith in a personal God.

The author of The Letter to the Hebrews describes Abraham as having turned his back upon traditions from which he came. Abraham was not thinking of that land from which he had gone out, and to which he had had opportunity to return if he had wanted to. But in his own inner sense of self-direction he did not choose to do so. He was like Moses, who chose voluntarily to suffer afflictions with the people of God rather than to enjoy the pleasures of the paganism of Egypt for a season. Abraham cast his lot with the people of God, as did Moses. Yet they were not determined by the people of God. They were not led by the quickly circling radar of what the people thought, but by a faith in God that was to them a pillar of fire by night and a pillar of cloud by day. The whole reason that they could do this was that they gained their sense of direction not from the worship of tradition, the idolatry of their own sense of mission, or obeisance to public opinion. They gained their sense of direction from a constantly renewed faith in a living God.

Under God the city they sought was not made with hands, could not be seen, and was not even readily apparent to them. They simply greeted the city of God from afar, acknowledged that they were strangers and pilgrims on earth, and knew that no earthly community they could build would be a lasting city, because they sought a city that was yet to come. Therefore, God was not ashamed to be called their God, and he prepared for them a city.

Faith is not a road map of other people's experience. It is not a gyroscope of self-sufficiency, confidence, and certainty. It is not a radarscope to pick up the commonly agreed on opinions of the group, for the group itself may be off course. Faith in God is like a seaman's sextant. The sextant keeps a person's direction true when he is out of sight of land or man. The stability of the universe, combined with the dedication of man, kept alive by the wisdom of the Creator through faith, helps us to maintain our position and chart our direction when all else is obscured or confusing. Our personal sense of selfhood is a kind of contract navigation whereby we may find our way. The traditions of our elders aid us in dead reckoning on the basis of previous voyagers' experience. The electronic navigation of radar brings us in touch with other voyagers on their way that we may confer with them. But faith comes to us through that celestial kind of navigation whereby we chart our course from the unconditional, unchanging, eternal character of the living God.

The faith of our fathers must be born anew in our own individuality. Otherwise, it becomes idolatry. Our individuality alone may be the elevation of ourselves without the knowledge that we are men and not God. Response to public opinion can be the worship of the crowd, and in all these instances we may be captured by the power of original sin. Any one of these taken as the main source of our direction leads to a false sense of security and may be a sheer attempt to take the uncertainty out of life. Thereby we deprive ourselves of the risk and adventure of the way of faith that God has prepared for us. And without a living, vital, personal faith in God through Christ, tradition becomes dead, self-identity becomes meaningless, and our awareness of a vital community disintegrates. Any of these as total security becomes a vain hope. Minnie Louise Haskins has said it most clearly in her little poem:

> And I said to the man who stood at the gate of the year:
> " Give me a light that I may tread safely into the un-
>   known! "
> And he replied:
> " Go out into the darkness and put your hand into the
>   Hand of God.
> That shall be to you better than light and safer than a
>   known way."

This was the courage of the Man of Galilee who went "outside the gate in order to sanctify the people through his own blood." We are called to follow him and to "go forth to him outside the camp." For, as the writer of The Letter to the Hebrews says, "We have no lasting city, but we seek the city which is to come."

THE DOUBLE COST
OF SPIRITUAL BLINDNESS

And they came to Bethsaida. And some people brought to him a blind man, and begged him to touch him. And he took the blind man by the hand, and led him out of the village; and when he had spit on his eyes and laid his hands upon him, he asked him, " Do you see anything? " And he looked up and said, " I see men; but they look like trees, walking." Then again he laid his hands upon his eyes; and he looked intently and was restored, and saw everything clearly. And he sent him away to his home, saying, " Do not even enter the village."

— Mark 8:22-26.

THE Master took the blind man by the hand and led him out of the pushing throng of the town to a place of quiet privacy. He laid his hands upon him after having moistened his eyes with saliva. Then he asked him if he could see. The man could only partially see. He could see men, he said, but they looked like walking trees. His vision was a bizarre distortion of the real world. The realm of men was a confused array of misimpressions. The therapy was incomplete, partial, and only well begun. A second touch of the Master was necessary before the distortions of vision could be clarified, before the man could see men as they really were.

This miracle is recorded only by Mark, the oldest of the Gospel records. Some scholars feel that the other biographers of our Lord left it out because it was not an instantaneous miracle, because it reveals process in healing, because it reflects human effort on the part of Jesus. Yet Mark saw no difficulty here that would cause him to delete the story. In including it, he tells us more about the human frailties of the man and the patient healing power of Jesus. The fact still remains that the *total* healing of many of our varied kinds of blindness calls for a second touch of the Master in order that our vision of man and of God may be clear.

For instance, I wonder if the placing of this healing story in the center of the instruction of Jesus concerning the bread and the cross is not significant in itself. The eighth chapter of Mark reveals Jesus wrestling with the blindness of more men than the blind man of Bethsaida. The disciples themselves were suffering from the same kind of blindness and hardness of heart as were the Pharisees. They had perceived the Kingdom of God as a material kingdom. Here they hoped safely to forget to bring bread by counting on the miraculous touch of Jesus to offset their error. Their blindness was carefully assessed by the Master Physician: " And being aware of it, Jesus said to them, ' Why do you discuss the fact that you have no bread? Do you not yet perceive or understand? Are your hearts hardened? Having eyes do you not see, and having ears do you not hear? ' "

Immediately after this discourse, Mark records the story of the healing of the blind man of Bethsaida. Then after this double touching of a blind man, Mark records the story of Jesus' great examination of the disciples. They confessed, with Peter as their spokesman, that he was the Christ. But still their vision of him was distorted. " And he began to teach them that the Son of man must suffer many things, and be rejected by the elders and the chief priests and the scribes, and be killed, and after three days rise again." Their blindness is revealed in Peter's tortured pleading that the cross not be so in the pilgrimage of the Christ. This confused perspective of the Christ, this twisted and misshapen condition of the disciples' vision, was nothing less than demonic to the steadfast and whole-viewed eye of Jesus. And he knew that if the eye is evil, the whole body will be full of darkness. " If then the light in you is darkness, how great is the darkness! " (Matt. 6:23.) Obviously the disciples, who had been with him so long, saw him as they did the scribes and Pharisees — " like trees, walking "! They had not heeded and learned to be aware of the leaven of the Pharisees. They needed the second touch of the Master as certainly as did the blind man of Bethsaida. The only difference was that their blindness was much more serious than his. Their awareness of it was much less acute. The cure of this blindness of theirs — and ours — would cost him his life!

Nevertheless, Jesus began to teach his disciples again about the Kingdom of God. Jesus is our " eternal contemporary " as he teaches that participation in the realm of redemption is not merely a search for pleasure and an avoidance of pain. The quest for a meaningful life involves a spiritual morality of loving risk. As Jesus put it: " If any man would come after me, let him deny himself and take up his cross and follow me. For whoever would save his life will lose it; and whoever loses his life for my sake and the gospel's will save it. For what does it profit a man, to gain the whole world and forfeit his life? " This teaching is the eye-opening truth of the gospel. It does not appear at first glance to those who embrace the Christian faith in order to " get something out " of religion. Nor does it appear to those who move on a calculated ethic of prudence that is supposed to make them more successful in every way. But until this second touch of the Master becomes vivid to a Christian, he is in a mist and darkness and has need of someone to lead him around by the hand.

Today, men desperately need the clarifying touch of the meaning and power of the Master's teaching of the cross as a way of life. This need, for instance, is particularly present in the success cults that form on every hand in the name of religion today. These sophisticated groups emphasize a material prosperity akin to that of the pious Jews of Jesus' day who saw Jesus as a miracle worker who could turn stones into bread and multiply the little into plenty. The main weakness of the gospels of success expounded by too many " popular " preachers is the fact that they consistently omit the reality of the cross as the way of life. Jesus preached and taught the conquering of death itself. Nevertheless, this caused the success-seeking throng to thin out.

Furthermore, individualistic groups of Christians often press for a verbal profession of faith. They usher a person into the church and into baptism. Often they do not pause to ask the person whether he really sees clearly the implications of what he has professed in becoming a Christian. This naturally is the result of much that passes for evangelism. The stumbling efforts of half-healed and half-helped persons who have depended upon the suggestive efforts of the revivalists must be dealt with again. Some other more patient person, concerned for the rootage and growth of the gospel, must refocus the convert's vision of life, of men, and of God. One of the common fallacies of vision found among new converts is that their profession of faith is supposed to solve all their problems and that their moods will always be elevated and happy ones. Consequently when a dark day, a bereavement, a disillusionment, a loneliness, a fear, comes upon them, they are likely to say that they are totally lost. Their vision of life is all confused, and they see men " like trees, walking." The second touch of the Master brings profounder light of the gospel on human suffering which makes of it a necessary part of creative living.

From a psychological point of view, the church has always been restless with popular distortions of psychological and religious interpretations of the gospel of grace. Popular thought has often twisted the doctrine of grace and freedom from legalism into occasion to gorge the desires of one's heart. For instance, the apostle Paul dealt with people who *heard* him say that they were free to " sin all the more in order that grace might abound." He hastens to say, " God forbid," and to point out in another connection that neither legalism (circumcision) nor freedom from the law (uncircumcision) avail anything, but only a new creation, a new being, in Christ.

Similar distortions have grown up today around psychotherapeutic interpretations of personality. Sigmund Freud, for instance, has been " used " as a justification for a purely pleasure-seeking, conscienceless way of life. Nothing could be farther from the truth, for he himself said that the conscious forces of personality should be enlightened with motives of love and should not be sacrificed in behalf of unbridled hostility and sexual drives.

In line with our theme, one can say that to see life as the search for pleasure and the avoidance of pain *only* is to be able only to half see, to move in a realm of distorted images and sense perceptions of a sensuous way of life. Sören Kierkegaard called a religion based on this view of life an " aesthetic " way of life. Such a religion views the cross as an object of a contemplation and sensuous beauty for the artist's brush and the poet's pen. Paul Tillich has accurately deplored this in American art wherein sentimentalism takes the place of the ethical demand and the threat of death implicit in any profound interpretation of the cross. This immaturity, when seen for what it is in the light of the instruction of Jesus as to the meaning of the cross, becomes more than immaturity: it becomes sin.

Furthermore, contemporary psychologists help us to clear up such popular distortions in which psychology is " used " as a justification for irresponsible hostility and sexuality. Gordon Allport, in his book *Becoming,* underlines the fact that the " propriate strivings " of men have far outweighed their desire for pleasure and the avoidance of pain in setting the pattern of their lives. By " propriate strivings," he means the kind of dedication that led Amundsen to explore the South Pole and to give up his life in attempting to rescue a comrade lost in the Arctic regions. Likewise, Gotthard Booth, a New York psychoanalyst, says that a man, be he atheist or Christian, has not achieved real security and health in life until he has a reason for living for which he is willing both to live and to die. Such a reason for living is larger than the bread-and-butter problem. Allport, again, calls it man's " longest-range intentions." Psychology is a young science. Contemporary psychologists such as Booth and Allport do not see men as walking trees; nor can they be used as justification for the half-sight of other men who still see men " like trees, walking."

When we study the workings of the human mind, we come upon another form of half-blindness wherein the second touch of the Master makes us " see life steadily and see it whole." Here our own sense of guilt and inner self-condemnation inflames our vision of other people. We see them as doing the things that secretly tempt us, and condemn them for it. This is called projection. Paul sensed this when he said that if we find a person in a fault, we should restore that person in a spirit of gentleness, lest we ourselves be tempted! It seems to be a law of the spirit that the more belligerent and intolerant we are toward someone, the more like that person we become. We see our own inner distortions in them. We see them " like trees, walking."

Now healing is the second touch of the Master upon the life of the person whose inner madness at himself, and all those who have made him what he is, enables him to move through an act of surrender of his grudge against life itself. He dies to this and is resurrected to walk in a new life. Then he sees for the first time clearly whereas he did see all his relationships to people in a distorted perspective.

Recently Jacqueline Cochran wrote her autobiography, *Stars at Noon*. You will possibly remember that she was the first woman aviator in a jet plane to break the sound barrier. She tells of climbing to an altitude of 53,000 feet in order to turn and make the dive. She says that as she moved upward and upward, her vision cleared. She moved out of the earthbound dust which refracted the perfect lights of heaven. Then she said that the gates of heaven are not brilliantly lighted. It is the dust of earth which refracts light and makes it hurt our eyes and makes it difficult for us to see. She says the heavens are a deep blue at noontide and you can see the stars at noon!

So it is in our vision of God — the multifarious cares and interferences of life hinder our vision of him and of one another. We see one another only painfully until he has touched our eyes again with the mystery of the Kingdom — a mystery that is revealed to babes but hidden to the wise and prudent. Then we are elevated to some transfiguration of our own when we see him as he is. " It does not yet appear what we shall be, but we know that when he appears we shall be like him, for we shall see him as he is "!

PURITY OF HEART
AND THE REVELATION OF GOD

Blessed are the pure in heart, for they shall see God.
— Matt. 5:8.

Religion that is pure and undefiled before God and the Father is this: to visit orphans and widows in their affliction, and to keep oneself unstained from the world.
— James 1:27.

THE revelation of God is obscured by the impurity of our hearts. Standing alone before God requires that we have " clean hands and a pure heart." As John Calvin has said, " 'to see God' is, in Palestinian speech, another way of saying ' appear before God.' " When a faithful Jew attended Temple worship, especially during the time of the great festivals, he suddenly became aware of various kinds of defilement that would disqualify him from " standing or appearing before the Lord." A clean heart was and is the prerequisite of acceptable worship before God. And for Jesus, as Calvin says, " *the* condition of having fellowship with God, here or hereafter, is a clean heart, a heart that loves goodness and hates evil." (John Calvin, *Harmony of Matthew, Mark, and Luke,* Vol. I, p. 264.)

As the prophet Isaiah, in the year that King Uzziah died, came into the Temple, he " saw the Lord . . . high and lifted up." Immediately he became aware of his own un-

clean lips, painfully conscious of the corporate guilt of the
people among whom he dwelt. He received a cleansing forgiveness from the altar of God and a challenging commission to prophesy to the people of God. In the process of his
commission he discovered his own whereabouts, his own
identity, and found his own sense of direction. As in his
case, the revelation of God to us calls for the suffering that
necessarily accompanies facing up to the inner distortions,
perversities, and sinfulness of our own hearts. In short, it
calls for purity of heart.

What Is Purity of Heart?

We have come to associate purity of heart merely with
the resistance of sexual temptation. But this is a corruption
of the Biblical understanding of purity of heart, although
this is not to say that the Biblical understanding does not
refer profoundly to the sexual temptations of man also. We
need, therefore, to explore the deeper recesses of the meaning of purity of heart as the Bible portrays it.

*Purity of heart means a concentration of the whole per-
sonality upon God as the center of our lives.* We have no
other gods before or beside him. Sören Kierkegaard, the
Danish poet-theologian of the last century, said that purity
of heart " is to will one thing, and that is Christ." He set
this over against the person who wills everything, avoiding
the necessity of making a choice among the many appeal-
ing claims upon his life. Jesus drew the distinction more
sharply when he said that we cannot serve two masters; we
will love the one and despise the other, or vice versa. Before Jesus, the prophet Elijah had confronted the people on
Mount Carmel with the choice between Baal and Yahweh.
He scorned them for " limping with two different opinions," saying, " If the Lord is God, follow him; but if Baal,

then follow him." In other words, purity of heart is the opposite of idolatry.

Spiritual adultery of an " evil and adulterous generation " in both the prophetic and the Christian sense of the words points directly to the flight of unfaithful worshipers to false gods. It is as Micah said of Samaria: " All her images shall be beaten to pieces, . . . and all her idols I will lay waste; for from the hire of a harlot she gathered them, and to the hire of a harlot they shall return " (Micah 1:7). And Paul also reminds the Galatian Christians that they had been " in bondage to beings that by nature are no gods." He roundly cautioned them how they were being tempted to "turn back again to the weak and beggarly elemental spirits " of their previous idolatry (Gal. 4:8 f.).

Present-day idolatry is much less obvious and more subtle than the gross fertility goddesses and agricultural deities of the days of Elijah. However, the subtlety of modern idolatry marks its strength. The thrust of its claim upon the imaginations of men is powered by its uncanny lack of obviousness. The idolatries of the sophisticated are much more entrenched than those of the primitive. Today idolatry moves in the inner recesses of our being and poisons the headsprings of our motivations. This makes the teachings of Jesus, therefore, all the more relevant to our situation.

As we have noted, William H. Whyte, Jr., in his book *The Organization Man,* strangely observes that the lust of modern men and women for security in a superorganization amounts to a " secular religion," a sort of faith in and of itself. To the contrary, others become self-styled " opponents " of the organization. In the name of freedom, they pawn their individuality, form crusades of their own, and in turn tyrannize those who do not agree with them. Frederick W. Robertson, commenting upon the labor movement in his day, said that labor leaders would become the "bloated aristocrats" of the twentieth century. In our generation of this century, labor itself has become capital. Our newspapers scream the story of how men's work has been made a commodity for the sake of the personal power of some labor leaders. The ambiguity of much that passes for a love of freedom and justice is reflected in the way in which the rebel becomes the tyrant.

What has been said here must not be interpreted as "beating the drum for capitalism" or as unappreciative of the hard-earned gains of mature and committed labor leaders. Rather, it is said in order to call attention to the way in which either capital or labor can become a form of idolatry, a way of life lived apart from the unifying power of direct obedience to the will of God. As Napoleon said, "vanity made the revolution; liberty was only a pretext."

Purity of heart, in the second place, means the reunion of the divided and fragmented self of a person; it means singleness of devotion, freedom from doubleness of mind in every sphere of life. Isaiah, pulled in every direction by the political currents of his troubled time, felt the overpowering conviction of his sin. He unified his heart in the resounding: "Here I am! Send me." He could say with the apostle Paul: "Not that I have already obtained this or am already perfect; but I press on to make it my own, because Christ Jesus has made me his own. Brethren, I do not consider that I have made it my own; but one thing I do, forgetting what lies behind and straining forward to what lies ahead, I press on toward the goal for the prize of the upward call of God in Christ Jesus" (Phil. 3:12-14).

In this context, Jesus' teachings about sexual lust emerge vividly into plain meaning. Just as spiritual faith required the unification of the whole personality around God, so the lover's love is adulterated, fragmented, and rendered insipid by dividing his or her loyalty. The rift of adulteration has begun when the look of lust sets in. The central meaning of adultery, then, is not merely the presence of sexual thoughts. This is typical of most healthy people. Rather, adultery is duplicity of devotion, the fragmentation of loyalty, and the disunity of commitment from the moment of its inception onward. Oneness of commitment and sincerity of heart in the love relationship between husband and wife are inseparable. The covenant of love is adulterated by deception, duplicity, and fear of exposure when lust begins.

Furthermore, emotional instability takes on a new meaning in the light of our interpretation of purity of heart as singleness of devotion. James speaks of the instability of the double-minded man in all his ways. John Bunyan describes the anxiety-ridden life of "Mr. Facing-both-ways." The double-minded man is like the partially covered and poorly bedded man of whom Isaiah spoke when he said the bed was too short to lie upon and the cover too narrow to be covered with. Observe the fretful restlessness of the person who anxiously tries to be covertly given to more than one God, more than one mate, more than one calling, more than one community of faith. He is like the person of whom Ephesians speaks, who is "tossed to and fro" by "every wind of doctrine" and the pressures of men. To the contrary, the person who "wills one thing" has a simplicity and depth that amounts to serenity even in the presence of the severest pressures. He, as the psalmist puts it, "swears to his own hurt and does not change." He is the person who "hath not lifted up his soul unto vanity, nor sworn deceitfully. He it is who is clean of hand and pure of heart" and may see God.

The anxiety that attends double-mindedness is the precondition of sin. This is the mosquito bed that breeds the maladies of the uncommitted and sinful life. To change the figure of speech, this indecision leaves life on our hands. We have to put it down somewhere when it gets too heavy. In other words, if we do not come to decisions and voluntarily commit ourselves to God and his calling for our lives, we are left in a passive position. We are involuntarily sucked into the vacuum of purposelessness created by our indecision. We are thus "led" into temptation by the way in which we have been created, that is, for singleness of heart, oneness of being, totality of response, completeness of commitment. As one writer has humorously put it in an anonymous poem:

> Within my earthly temple there's a crowd:
> There's one of us that's humble, one that's proud,
> There's one that's brokenhearted for his sins,
> And one that's unrepentant sits and grins.
> There's one that loves his neighbor as himself,
> And one that cares for naught but fame and pelf,
> From much perplexing care I would be free
> If I could once determine which is me!

In this sense, then, impurity of heart is not the *result* of wrongdoing, but the cause of wrongdoing. The basic indecisiveness and inability to determine "which is me," "who I am," *breeds* perplexing care and wrong action.

Then, again, in the third place, purity of heart means having clear motives for doing the work of God. Jesus illustrated the centrality of this meaning of purity of heart in the succeeding words of the Sermon on the Mount. He urged his disciples not to be like the hypocrites, who gave their alms to be seen of men, who disfigured their faces when they fasted, and who prayed long prayers for the effect upon others. James, also, defined "pure religion and undefiled before God " in terms of a direct ministry to orphans and widows. Immediately, however, he cautioned against doing these things for motives "spotted by the world."

Lance Webb, in his book *Discovering Love,* tells the story of a prominent society woman who asked a social worker how she might be helpful to the poor children of New York. She wrote a long letter telling how she hoped her service to the children would help her to make up for some of her own shortcomings. Webb quotes the letter (from Joshua Loth Liebman's book *Peace of Mind*), which the candid social worker wrote to the socialite:

> Dear Madam, Your truly magnificent shortcomings at present are too great. Nothing could prevent you from visiting them on victims of your humility. I advise you to love yourself more before you squander any love on others.

This penetrating and sardonic wisdom cuts through much of the sentimentality that is mistaken for love. It calls for a cauterizing analysis of our reasons for righteousness. The New Testament helps us in making such an analysis of our love for self, others, and God. The law of survival says that we should love our neighbor and hate our enemies. The prudential ethic of the pious Jew says that we should do unto others as we would have them do unto us. The great commandment of prophetic wisdom says that we should love our neighbors as ourselves. The Jewish understanding of Liebman underscores the fact that we actually do love others in proportion to our basic self-respect and regard. However, the transmoral ethic of the Lord Jesus Christ gives us a new commandment: "that we love one another as he has loved us." Thus, we no longer see one another from a human point of view but as persons "for whom Christ died." His redemptive act in death, burial, and resurrection becomes the cleansing motive for doing the work of God.

One of the truly helpful contributions that modern psychology has made to the religious life of Christians is to help us evaluate more realistically the motives we have for doing religious work. The demand for an enduring responsibility to examine our hearts rests upon us from the beginning of Biblical revelation to the end. The tools for doing this have been made available to us in more detail by scientific research. We know that we can be interested in orphans and widows, for instance, for motives far afield from that of bringing to them the good news of Jesus Christ. We can be concerned about them for their property, for after all the Scripture speaks of the exploitation of widows too. We can be concerned about orphans because of our own need to rule a person who is weaker than ourselves. Subtle needs to serve them in order to gratify frustrations of our own rather than to serve them for their own sakes may easily creep into our motives. Purity of heart in service of any kind calls for rigid self-examination. As we examine our hearts, God reveals himself to us in the inner chambers of being.

The clinical pastoral training of theological students today in the majority of our theological seminaries reflects the importance of such purification of the motives of the minister through the processes of his education. Students are placed in a supervised and controlled setting for ministering to others, such as a hospital, a child-care or penal institution. The whole process of education consists in carefully exploring with the student the motives of his ministry to needy persons, and clarifying the intentions behind his good works. The words of the mouth and the meditations of the heart are driving forces of the works of our hands. We feel as ministers that under God both student and teacher should submit himself to careful examination of our ministry of the word of God to the sick, the confused, the needy, the outcast. These " little ones of his " deserve to be treated as " persons for whom Christ died " and not as means to our own self-chosen and unexamined ends. Seeing God in the sufferings of stress-ridden people itself calls for purity of heart on our part. For that matter, laying hold of our own sufferings as an instrument of ministry to others demands that we ourselves shall have come to a clear-eyed understanding of our own sufferings first. Otherwise, we are the blind leading the blind.

WHAT IS SPIRITUAL SIGHT AND BLINDNESS?

The fact remains, however, that some people prefer darkness to light, erect the imaginations of their own hearts in such a way that they become " high things " that exalt themselves against the knowledge of God and obscure the revelation of God. God warned Isaiah that the very attempt to communicate the revelation of God to some people would make their hearts fat, their ears heavy, and their eyes shut. This is the antithesis of seeing God through the cleansing of the heart, the sensitizing of the ear, and the opening of the eyes. John Calvin says that this is accidental to and not a necessary part of the preaching of the Word of God. In a sense it is like thrusting a great light into a person's eyes after his have been in darkness all his life. He will be like those of whom Plato speaks in his allegory of the cave. When they were released from the darkness of their bondage in the cave and led out into the brilliant light of the spangled heavens of reality, they ran back into the darkness because of the pain to their eyes. This is such an important truth in the Scriptures that the passage from Isaiah to which reference has just been made is repeated six times in the New Testament. A person gets to the point that sweet is bitter, light is darkness, good is evil, evil is good, and no longer is his yea, yea, and his nay, nay. As Ralph Waldo Emerson has said, " when simplicity of character . . . is broken up by the prevalence of secondary desires, and duplicity and falsehood take the place of simplicity and truth, the power over nature as an interpreter of the will is in a degree lost." (Ralph Waldo Emerson, in *Complete Essays and Other Writings*. Modern Library.)

Yet, in our sentimental and unrealistic conceptions of the Christian faith, we cannot absorb this sterner side of the beautiful Beatitude that the pure in heart shall see God. We gag at the thought that people *can,* as Calvin says, in the presence of the light of God " sufficient to light all the senses, . . . maliciously darken themselves." (John Calvin, in *Commentary on Acts,* Vol. II, p. 429.) Some interpreters of the Scripture go even farther and say that God elects to harden some hearts against his revelation of himself. But the wrath of God always works through the voluntary responses of the choosing person, even as also does his love. The hardening of the heart, the dimming of the vision, habitually chosen, becomes a reality that is well nigh if not actually irreversible. There is a point of no return in spiritual resistance and inner idolatry.

THE URGENCY OF GOD'S REVELATION

Therefore, the claims of the Christian faith are clear that " this day " is the day of salvation. The persistent challenge of the Lord Jesus Christ to our idolatry, our halfheartedness and our mixed motives cannot be temporized with, put off to another day, or considered as some new thing to be set over against another enchanting idea. We are called upon to cast down " every high thing that exalted itself against the knowledge of God " and to give unto the Christ a name that is " above every name," confessing him as Lord in our lives. We are caught in the throes of our limping indecisiveness and challenged to a " singleness of heart " that comes as a gift of grace upon faith in Christ. We are set forth upon a lifelong path of growth through the simplification and purification of our motives for good works for which we were created that we should do them.

ANGER, SUFFERING,
AND THE REVELATION OF GOD

Therefore, putting away falsehood, let every one speak the truth with his neighbor, for we are members one of another. Be angry but do not sin; do not let the sun go down on your anger, and give no opportunity to the devil. . . . Let all bitterness and wrath and anger and clamor and slander be put away from you, with all malice, and be kind to one another, tenderhearted, forgiving one another, as God in Christ forgave you.
— Eph. 4:25-27, 31-32.

THE kindling of a man's wrath both hides God from the man and reveals God to the man. This is so because we come face to face with ourselves in our anger in ways unknown to us in the presence of other emotions. Moses' anger waxed hot against the Egyptian slavemaster whipping the Israelites. Having fled from the punishment for his murder of the Egyptian, he had many years to contemplate his act in the lonely wilderness until he came face to face with God to a bush that burned and was not consumed.

Men could not hate one another if they did not deeply want to be like one another. Their love curdles into jealousy. Their hatred causes them to " breathe out threatenings and slaughters " against one another. But just at this crucial moment, men had better be careful lest some blinding and converting revelation of the eternal God in Christ thrust them into a new relationship to themselves, to God, and to their fellow man. Yet, it is amazing how careful men who will not be reconciled can be at such a moment to avoid the revelations of the Eternal. These insights remain forever a closed mystery to them as their anger settles into aversion, and their aversion into a grudging, paranoid pattern of life. Thus men, as Emily Dickinson says, "erect defences against love's violence."

What, then, is the Biblical witness for the Christian when he gets angry? This we must know because the most painful sufferings we have to bear come in our conflicts with other Christians. Is there any revelation to be found in these sufferings? We cannot just be pious, sentimental, and sirupy here. We must have some clear leading. We turn to the Biblical revelation for it.

ANGER AND THE PRACTICE OF SPIRITUAL DIRECTNESS

The Biblical witness reflects an understanding permissiveness about getting angry. Jesus affectionately nicknamed James and John "Boanerges," which comes from a combination of Aramaic terms meaning "tumultuous" and "thunderous anger." They were "sons of thunder." Yet, as J. B. Weatherspoon has pointed out, James later became the quiet and controlled executive of the early church, and John the tenderhearted and beloved disciple of great gentleness. These men, in their youth, though, were the ones who wanted to call down fire upon the heads of an inhospitable Samaritan village for its discourtesy to their teacher Jesus. They were like untamed stallions unbroken to the harness of the discipleship into which Christ had called them. But, as someone has said, it is easier to tame and discipline a bucking stallion that it is to put fire into a dull, dead, and spiritless dray horse! Such was the permissive and yet farseeing insight of Jesus in the selection of thunderously angry James and John.

The New Testament witness encourages and even demands the practice of directness in the expression of anger. We see this in the behavior of the leaders of the early church. For example, Paul tells us, in Gal. 2:11 ff., that when Peter came to Antioch, he, Paul, " opposed him to his face because he stood condemned. For before certain men came from James, he ate with the Gentiles; but when they came he drew back and separated himself, fearing the circumcision party. And with him the rest of the Jews acted insincerely, so that even Barnabas was carried away by their insincerity. But when I saw that they were not straightforward about the truth of the gospel, I said to Cephas before them all, 'If you, though a Jew, live like a Gentile and not like a Jew, how can you compel the Gentiles to live like Jews?'" Here Paul forthrightly expressed his displeasure in face-to-face encounter with the apostle Peter with whom he disagreed.

Another example appears in Paul's dealings with Barnabas. They had had some sort of an unpleasant experience with Mark on an earlier missionary journey, and he had turned back from them. On a later journey, described in Acts, ch. 15, Barnabas " wanted to take with them John called Mark. But Paul thought best not to take with them one who had withdrawn from them in Pamphylia, and had not gone with them to the work. And there arose a sharp contention, so that they separated from each other." We do not know all the details of these encounters. For instance, we do not know what the apostle Peter or Barnabas said; we have only one side of the account. We do know that Paul and Barnabas had other contacts that were pleasant, and that Paul recognized the worth of Mark in his later years. But in both instances we have shimmeringly bright examples of Christians in the early church who had sharp disagreements and expressed their anger directly.

We get a key to the problem, however, when we read the Ephesian letter in which the author says, " Be angry but do not sin." This is not simply a matter of " loving the sinner and hating his sin," as the trite aphorism puts it. To the contrary, it is being open and transparent rather than sweetly covert and deceptive about one's feelings. We have a colloquial phrase that describes it aptly. We say that we are " leveling with " a person with whom we disagree. Otherwise, he senses the traction and withdrawal of spirit and becomes suspicious of us and we of him. This is giving place and opportunity to the devil who enters to distort, confuse, misrepresent, and multiply discord.

QUICKNESS OF RECONCILIATION AND FORGIVENESS

The permissiveness of the New Testament writers about the expression of anger is matched by their equal insistence upon a quick eagerness for reconciliation in tenderhearted forgiveness. Popular interpreters of psychology have stressed the importance of self-expression, the way in which repressed, unrecognized, and unaccepted hostilities can damage the life-impulse of a person, and the necessity of direct release of anger. Undisciplined and irresponsible persons have often justified their lack of self-discipline with such teachings. They have, as a result, taken hard-earned psychological wisdom and perverted it into a sort of " psychology of the splurged urge."

The New Testament probes this insight more deeply and couples the practice of " leveling " or " directness " with a demand for an equally necessary eagerness for reconciliation. In Ephesians, where we are encouraged to " be angry," we are in the same breath told " not to let the sun go down on our anger." We are urged not to give even one night's sleep an opportunity to fester an anger into a resentment, a resentment into a settled aversion, or a settled aversion into a grudge, or a grudge into a paranoid sense of persecution.

Paul pictures this quickness of reconciliation and eagerness to forgive in terms of a childlikeness toward life. You have seen children who are playing suddenly become angry with one another. Often, before an adult can get to them to " straighten them out," they are friends again. As Paul said, " Brethren, be not children in understanding: howbeit in malice be ye children . . ." (I Cor. 14:20). Such was the wisdom also of Jesus when he urged that we agree with our adversary quickly, while we are in the way with him; for to fail to do so is to pay and pay and pay until we have paid the last farthing.

TENDERNESS OF HEART AND FORGIVENESS OF OPPONENTS

Quickness of reconciliation is rooted and grounded in truth and love. We are to speak the truth directly to our brother and be eager for reconciliation. But we are to " speak the truth in love " if we are to grow up into Christ who is the head of the church. As O. T. Binkley has said, if we restricted what we have to say to those things which are spoken as truth in love, we would cut down the amount that we have to say to a tenth, but the strength of our utterance would be multiplied tenfold. We would have much less to say, and it would be far more worth-while to hear!

Furthermore, eager reconciliation is hastened by tenderness of heart. Gentleness springs from an acute awareness of our own shortcomings, our infinite dependence upon God for forgiveness, and our deep sense of necessity for fellowship with our estranged brother, friend, and neighbor. The apostle Paul says that when we have overtaken a brother in a fault, we should restore him with a spirit of gentleness, looking to ourselves, lest we also be tempted. Our contempt for an offender is often rooted in our own struggles in temptation with the very thing we condemn in him. Whether we call this " projection," as the psychologists do, " hypocrisy," as the New Testament does, or " original sin," as the Calvinist does, we are dealing with the same streak of self-deception in human nature. Our harshness springs from our inner blindness to our own anger at ourselves.

But, when the "eyes of our inner understanding are opened," we can be tenderhearted and forgiving of one another, because we have a deep sense of having been forgiven ourselves. We are not driven by our own unconscious guilts into despising another, desecrating his personality, and offering ourselves up on the altar of hatred for him. For such hatred is idolatry, an idolatry that centers our lives around a person whom we despise to the point of self-destruction, a perverted act of suicide of one kind or another.

But the Christian will not allow another man to destroy him by permitting himself to hate him. He puts away falsehood and speaks directly the truth with his neighbor. He does so in love and in such a way as to edify and not to destroy his neighbor. But, more than this, he lets all bitterness and wrath and anger and slander be put away from him, along with all malice, and insists upon being kind, tenderhearted, and forgiving, as God in Christ forgave him. These are the heights of magnanimity that the forgiven Christian reaches in his handling of his anger. They are heights based upon the rock of God's forgiveness and not upon a self-sufficiency or a pride of spirit.

Hatred and the Unpardonable Sin

Much speculation has gone into guessing about the exact character of the unpardonable sin. However, we come very near to the heart of the meaning of the unpardonable sin in our discussion of the angers and hatreds of the Christian. The simple fact remains that many Christians carry unresolved and unmet grudges in their hearts that have become the organizing center of their lives. They have dedicated themselves as if to a calling to hate some particular person, group of persons, or institutions. They are possessed by the power of the hatred which they cherish, nourish, and keep alive each waking moment and fan with their dreams into deeper life each night. They are as the elder brother upon hearing the rejoicing of his father and friends over the return of the prodigal son: " . . . he was angry and refused to go in."

We usually look in the more obscure passages of The Letter to the Hebrews for the meaning of the unpardonable sin, but at the same time we carefully avoid the plain teaching of the Sermon on the Mount in which Jesus says, " For if you forgive men their trespasses, your heavenly Father also will forgive you; but if you do not forgive men their trespasses, neither will your Father forgive your trespasses " (Matt. 6:14-15).

This is the hardness of heart that grieves the teaching of the Holy Spirit and alienates men from themselves, from one another, and from fellowship with God. This is the final test of the validity of our birth into new life in Christ. For, as I John 3:14 puts it, " we know that we have passed out of death into life, because we love the brethren."

The early church had much experience in dealing with anger, conflict, railings, slander, and so forth. They devised a fourfold formula for dealing with such misunderstandings, failures of communication, abortions of the new birth, and arrestings of spiritual maturity. In Matt., ch. 18, we have a recorded teaching of Jesus that they applied to such necessities in their " life together." First, they " practiced directness," and if a brother sinned against a man, the offended person would go quietly to him and tell him his fault, a matter between themselves alone. If the offender refused to listen, a Christian brother would then go along, in order that whatever was said might be heard by another person and that by his counsel he might be able to hasten reconciliation. If this failed, they brought the matter out into public and the community as a whole sought to effect reconciliation. When this failed, they considered that the person had not even been won from among the pagans. He should be treated as a person who yet needs changing, conversion to the Christian way. In this context, Jesus is quoted as having said, " If two of you agree on earth about anything they ask, it will be done for them by my Father in heaven " (Matt. 18:19).

Unresolved conflicts with others create blockages of the prayer life and hinder the revelation of God. Deep agreement between estranged men and women looses their spiritual energies for creative achievement and spiritual discovery so great that " eye hath not seen, nor ear heard," the things that are waiting to be revealed to the Christians who will take seriously the mind of Christ.

Many times the source of anger-generating conflict lies in plain misunderstanding and failure of communication. The two persons are operating from different sets of information, and their conflict naturally results. The pooling of their knowledge quite often throws new light on their perspectives and enables them to understand each other. The

Holy Spirit is always at work in the creation of a total view of any given situation, as has been said, helping people to " see life steadily and see it whole." Quick, face-to-face conference with the person against whom we are offended makes this possible.

But we do err when we assume that all misunderstanding arises from failures of communication. Many times, as in the case of the apostle Peter and the apostle Paul, fundamental disagreements do exist. Men's basic understanding of the character of the covenant of the Christian faith is not the same. In such instances, we must go back to the fundamental principles on which the disagreement turns and grasp the basic issues that transcend our personal differences, our own struggles for power, and our own security operations and defenses. Then the test of our Christian maturity is our ability to live and work with and learn from a person with whom we basically disagree. This is the supreme criterion of the mature Christian at the point of his handling his angers, hostilities, and resentments. In this balance of Christian ethics we must weigh ourselves and see if we are found wanting.

THE GRIEF OF THE UPROOTED

> By the waters of Babylon,
>   there we sat down and wept,
>   when we remembered Zion.
> On the willows there
>   we hung up our lyres.
> For there our captors
>   required of us songs,
> and our tormentors, mirth, saying,
>   " Sing us one of the songs of Zion! "
>
> How shall we sing the Lord's song
>   in a foreign land? — Ps. 137:1-4.

THE Jews had been ruthlessly torn up from their native land and taken as prisoners of war to Babylon. Their humiliating defeat was rubbed raw by the separation from their homes and from the holy Temple of Zion. Had not they always gone here to " see God," to await with breathless expectation the breaking through of the brilliance of the Lord from the Holy of Holies? Now, uprooted from the very dwelling place of the Most High God, they were homesick believers.

THE SORROW OF UPROOTING

Both the poignant grief and the piercing question of these homesick believers in the Lord are the suffering of many uprooted persons today. The same kind of prison camp, ghetto, and concentration of displaced persons has happened on such a scale in our day as to make the exile of the Jews seem like a small thing. The Nationalists of China have been driven from their homes to Formosa. Great hordes of prisoners of war of World War II and the Korean conflict have never found their way back home. They have been thrust into strange and hostile environments, far from the temples of their native worship. Displaced persons have come to this country seeking work, livelihood, and new opportunity. Nevertheless, they have an inner wistfulness of the spirit for the accustomed ways of life, the known hymns of their native lands. They wonder how they can sing the songs of the Lord in a strange land.

Even apart from war and imprisonment, individuals and families are " on the move." Twenty-one million or more Americans change their residences each year. It is nothing unusual in a suburban church community to have ten to fifteen families " transferred " at one time by their company. The military establishments of our country keep large numbers of families in a constant state of readiness to move. As a person travels through the country, he is impressed by the number of trailer villages that have sprung up, symbolizing the rootlessness of the lives of a growing migrant population. Government workers in a city, for instance, like Washington, D.C., live under the pressure of the possibility of the " change of an administration." Consequently, they always think of themselves as being " away from home." Everyone is from somewhere else other than Washington!

Consider also the uprooted lives of adolescent boys and girls in college and for the first time away from home. Here they meet other boys and girls from all over the world.

Their provincial ideas are challenged by the presence of people with names, dialects, complexions, and beliefs different from their own. This is indeed the age of uprooting for them. They must lengthen the cords and strengthen the stakes of their understanding of God, Christ, and the church. They may feel that they are " losing their religion," and that their faith is shaken. With wise guidance they can be uprooted and planted afresh in a larger faith. To change the figure, they can shed the milk-grown baby teeth of the religion of their childhood and allow room for the meat-grown adult teeth of a religion of maturity to take their place.

However, this is not the only possibility. They may grow up to be young intellectuals in every respect except their religious faith. They may even reject their whole religious heritage. They may become those lonely persons, the modern-day " lost sheep of the house of Israel," who, like Thomas Wolfe, " can't go home again." They become captives of a permanent sense of exile, so well expressed by Wolfe when he said " that men are strangers, that they are lonely and forsaken, that they are in exile on this earth, that they are born, live, and die alone." (*The Letters of Thomas Wolfe,* ed. by Elizabeth Nowell, Charles Scribner's Sons, 1956, p. 216.) They begin to pray inwardly, as did Wolfe, " for something outside of me to last."

The most heartening experience of my own pastoral ministry has been to break through the isolation and loneliness that possesses many a veteran professional person as well as rebellious young research men and scientists, and discover a spiritual wistfulness of stringent loneliness of being. They have gone beyond the point of no return to the quaint and unsophisticated simplicity of religious belief of their childhood. Yet, they have not found in their vocation anything but competition, demands for almost ascetic discipline, and the few crumbs of gratitude given to them by the one out of ten persons they help who return to say thanks. They long for a " filial relation with the cosmos which has begotten them . . .," as Gardner Murphy so aptly puts it. The Christian pastor and the community of faith that he represents have only dimly begun to become aware of the suffering involved in the spiritual homesickness of the average professionally and scientifically trained person.

When a person is uprooted he is profoundly affected. He may become homesick to the core of his being. He may be like the five-year-old son of a friend of mine who moved away from the neighborhood in which he had been living. The little fellow was sad to tears for having to leave his playmates. As they were moving into the new home, he said to his father: " Daddy, we need to have a little room in our house specially for prayer so we will have a place to go in times like these! " Similarly I recall having left home at the age of thirteen to become a page in the United States Senate. I remember the spirit of heaviness, the lump in my throat, the sheer loneliness of the dark room I occupied all by myself, and the way in which I counted the days of my first year there.

Such homesickness of the spirit strikes deeply when we consider our separation, isolation, and being cut off from our known and accustomed time, place, and manner of worship of God. We come easily to associate God with the place where we, according to our custom, have habitually worshiped him. Even Jesus found comfort in returning to his home town of Nazareth and worshiping in his home synagogue, " as his custom was." The Jews of the captivity before him had prayed that their right hand would wither and that their tongue would cleave to the roof of their mouth if they forgot the joy and necessity of Jerusalem for their worship of God.

But other Jews were not so piously eager to remember Jerusalem. They, to the contrary, " walked in the counsel of the wicked," " stood in the way of sinners," and " sat in the seat of scoffers." Apparently, they were both delighted to be away from the restrictions of their home community, and at the same time desperately eager to " enjoy the pleasures of sin for a season." They were like many uprooted people today who take a spiritual moratorium when away from home. When at home they are pious, self-respecting, and respected people, but when away from home the source of their morality, that is, the external approval of those who know them, is gone. The church membership of many people remains in their home town although they themselves have not been there for decades. Their participation in the way and work of God is deferred until that nebulous time when they will go back to the old home place. The loosening of moral and spiritual roots in our highly mobile culture has caused the inner growth and outer fruit to wither and fail.

Underneath both the homesickness and the withering of the spiritual life associated with uprooting lies the subtle conviction that God is restricted to a certain piece of geography, that he is not accessible in Babylon but only in Jerusalem. Such a religion is little better than the religion of the Romans who worshiped their household gods. The Jew may be like the Britisher of whom one of his critics said, " To him, God is another Britisher nine feet tall! " Or, along a more serious vein, people are like Naaman, who was healed by Elisha. He then wanted to take two mules' burden of earth back to Syria with him, obviously in order that he might worship the God of the ground on which he had stood when Elisha had brought healing to him from the Lord.

THE REVELATION OF A UNIVERSAL GOD

But the great spiritual discovery of the exile of the Jews came when they found that God was in Babylon as well as in Jerusalem. They discovered him as a God who "has measured the waters in the hollow of his hand and marked off the heavens with a span, enclosed the dust of the earth in a measure and weighed the mountains in scales and the hills in a balance" (Isa. 40:12). He was the Holy One of Israel, but "the whole earth was full of his glory." He was no tribal deity, nor a household god, nor a local idol. The Lord became to them an everlasting God, the "Creator of the ends of the earth." They had hitherto seen him in his all-powerfulness; now they found him out in his ever-presence throughout the whole earth.

Such was the revelation that Jesus brought forcefully home in the conversation with the woman at the well. She raised the whole question that separated the competing religious worship of the Samaritans and the Jews. She wanted to know his position: did he worship at Mt. Gerizim or at Jerusalem? He also felt the harsh inhospitality of a Samaritan village at another time when they rejected him because he was headed toward Jerusalem for worship. Some of the historical research students of the Scripture say that the re-called words of Jesus in response to the woman at the well were actually recorded *after* the destruction of Jerusalem and Gerizim! All the more apropos, then, were his words:

> Woman, believe me, the hour is coming when neither on this mountain nor in Jerusalem will you worship the Father. . . . The hour is coming, and now is, when the

> true worshipers will worship the Father in spirit and
> truth, for such the Father seeks to worship him. God is
> spirit, and those who worship him must worship in spirit
> and truth. (John 4:21, 23-24.)

In the breaking up of our overdependence upon family,
tradition, custom, and geography, God reveals to us in the
midst of this painful suffering his eternal, universal, spiritual, and omnipresent character. Out of the stress and strain
of our homesickness and temptation to laxness and cynicism
is born a transforming new understanding of the nature
and character of God!

With such a spiritually inexhaustible source of creative
power in a living God who is available everywhere, we are
renewed day by day, regardless of our locality. He goes
with us as the One who " does not faint or grow weary."
He stands by to strengthen us as he did the apostle Paul
when he was in prison. He brings new life to the plantings
of our lives, even though they are uprooted. As Briggs translates Ps. 1:3, such a righteous person is " like a tree transplanted by the streams of water." This person, in spite of
the transplanting, brings forth fruit without missing a
season, without even a leaf withering!

Here we may return to the life of Thomas Wolfe and
others who " have gone beyond the point of no return," who
are spiritual orphans and " can't go home again." Abraham
was similarly cut off from his home in Ur of the Chaldees.
The main difference was that he *could* have returned if he
had wanted to return. He had not left out of compulsive
desire to get away, but readily, by faith. As The Letter to the
Hebrews says, he and other men of faith " acknowledged
that they were strangers and exiles on the earth." The
author of this letter further points out that " if they had
been thinking of that land from which they had gone out,

they would have had opportunity to return." But the fact of the matter was that they " desired a better country. . . . Therefore God . . . has prepared for them a city." This, then, is the difference between handling our age with anxiety and handling it with faith. We voluntarily through faith in God leave father, mother, house, lands, and all our most cherished attachments and " desire a better country, that is, a heavenly one." We do not return home because of the onward pull of the Kingdom of God, not because we are filled with unresolved hostilities and fears about our native homes. We have taken roots in the greatness of God!

One of the truly reassuring impressions of this generation is to see just this kind of thing happening in the lives of American soldiers and their families who are scattered to the four corners of the earth today. Quite often we see them laying hold of the inner resources of their fellowship with God and beginning small churches, caring for the spiritual needs of war orphans, strengthening already existing missionary endeavors of the various churches, and encouraging their fellow soldiers in a vital experience of the Christian faith. Colonel Julia E. Hamblet, Director of the Women Marines, tells of having heard late at night as she was inspecting the women's barracks at Parris Island, S.C., the blowing of taps. Usually great quiet follows the last bugle note. But on this occasion, the young voices of the women recruits blended together in the singing of The Lord's Prayer. Colonel Hamblet said: " They were not required to sing. They did so because they chose to." They no longer needed the piano in the family living room or the organ in the sanctuary of their home church. The barracks had become the dwelling place of the Lord in prayer.

" How shall we sing the Lord's song in a strange land? " By discovering that " they who wait for the Lord shall renew their strength," that he is always nigh, and that he is closer than hands and feet, nearer than breathing. "Where two or three are gathered in his name, there he is in the midst of them," and they can make their petitions known unto him and be heard by him. This becomes the foundation of the moral life, the headspring of spiritual growth and productivity.

GOD, THE REDEEMER OF ALL MANKIND

When we discover that God is universal and ever-present, we then come face to face with him as the redeemer of all mankind and not a private possession of our own clan or race. We leap the barriers of our own provincialism, and the middle wall of partition, which separates us from accepting and understanding people of different color, custom, and clan from us, is torn down. We are lifted up, as was the apostle Peter, into a vision of a God who is " no respecter of persons," one who has not made any man common or unclean. We discover our kinship even with our captors, as was true of the apostle Paul in the house of Caesar. The restricting circles that we have drawn to shut others out are encompassed by the larger and ever-enlarging circle of the love of God for all his creation. This was the astounding revelation to the woman at the well who could not understand how it was that Jesus, being a Jew, could speak to her, a Samaritan woman. The old wineskins of the confines of the Jewish faith were too small to hold the new wine of his revelation of God as the redeemer of all men of all the world.

Missionary enthusiasm is in direct proportion to the vision of God that grips us. One of the great tragedies of the present day is the shattering of the securities of a known community of people who are accustomed to one another's ways. But we cannot, without risking the worst idolatry of all and without distorting the very revelation of the character of God himself, depend upon such safety mechanisms for our spiritual creativity and productivity. This can be blasted away from us in a moment's time. We have no enduring city here. We must seek a family of God that transcends blood ties, a home that reaches beyond our own city limits, and a city whose builder and maker is God, eternal in the mind and purpose of God. We must sink our rootage into the greatness of God in order that we may, even though we are transplanted, bring forth fruit in our due season and in order that our leaf may not wither. Then, as the Revelator says, " the leaves of the tree shall be for the healing of the nations."

CHAPTER

13

PARENTHOOD AND THE
NECESSITY FOR SUFFERING

And he will turn many of the sons of Israel to the Lord their
  God,
and he will go before him in the spirit and power of Elijah,
to turn the hearts of the fathers to the children.
— Luke 1:16-17.

"For this reason a man shall leave his father and mother
and be joined to his wife, and the two shall become one." This
is a great mystery, and I take it to mean Christ and the church;
however, let each one of you love his wife as himself, and
let the wife see that she respects her husband.

Children, obey your parents in the Lord, for this is right.
"Honor your father and mother," (this is the first commandment with a promise), "that it may be well with you
and that you may live long on the earth." Fathers, do not provoke your children to anger, but bring them up in the discipline and instruction of the Lord.
— Eph. 5:31 to 6:4.

THE power struggle between adults, all of whom are
weakened sinners before God, kicks up so much dust
that the revelation of God is obscured. This is what happened when the disciples came to Jesus, saying to him,
"Who is the greatest in the kingdom of heaven?" We are
told that Jesus then called to him a child, "put him in the
midst of them, and said, 'Truly, I say to you, unless you
turn and become like children, you will never enter the

kingdom of heaven. . . . See that you do not despise one
of these little ones; for I tell you that in heaven their angels
do always behold the face of my Father who is in heaven ' "
(Matt. 18:1-3, 10). Our Lord is telling us that in the face
of little children we may behold the revelation of God, find
a pattern for life and a stance of the mind that, if taken,
requires our full conversion. Such a conversion means turning away from our power struggle and setting our face
toward the entrance to the Kingdom of Heaven.

Set high on one side of Riverside Drive in New York
City is the tomb of Ulysses S. Grant. It is a mammoth structure, filled with relics of war, and set forth in true honor
and memory of a great warrior and general. However, on
the other side of Riverside Drive, literally tucked away and
out of sight in the heavy foliage of the park, is another
grave. It is the grave of five-year-old St. Clair Pollock, " an
amiable child." Since 1797 it has been faithfully cared for
and tended by the park attendants. One of these graves
symbolizes the power struggles for greatness that issue in
war between men. The other symbolizes the way the spirit
of God in Christ turns our hearts back to little children. In
doing so, he turns us back to himself and reveals the essential character of the Godhead to us.

The visitant of the Lord stood on the right side of the
altar of incense and spoke to Zacharias about the coming
of his son, John the Baptist. He said of John the Baptist,
" He will turn many of the sons of Israel to the Lord their
God, and he will go before him in the spirit and power of
Elijah, to turn the hearts of the fathers to the children." The
theme of this sermon is that in the parent-child relationship,
God breaks through to us, turning the hardness of our
hearts into tender adoration and making himself known in
the face of a little child.

In no other arena of human existence do tragedy and triumph, suffering and birth, less than a breath's distance from each other, more vividly reveal the real presence of the living Christ than in the parent-child relationship. We do well, therefore, to look here also for the appearing of God. The drama of God's revelation of himself moves from stage to stage along life's way in every family's spiritual pilgrimage.

PARENTHOOD DEMANDS CHANGE

In the first place, we can say that God's redeeming love is revealed in the vast changes that are demanded of mother and father by the birth of a child into their home. Parents are made to ask transforming questions of themselves. This is a time of deep spiritual awakening, searching, and turning. The birth of a child into a home is potentially — although not necessarily — a worship experience. We are confronted with the mystery of creativity. We are overwhelmed with the awe-inspiring awareness that a Power not our own has been at work. We are caused to remember what our own parents have done for, with, and to us. We are thrust into the kind of prayer that Manoah, the father of Samson, prayed when he "entreated the Lord, and said, 'O, Lord, I pray thee let the man of God whom thou didst send come again to us, and teach us what we are to do with the boy that will be born.'"

Little wonder, then, is it that at the decisive time of becoming parents, husbands and wives are thrust into a new spiritual era! God's redeeming love is either revealed or concealed by the vast changes that are demanded of them as mother and father. The experience of a young psychiatrist is not unlike that of many young parents. He said that during his late teen-age years and during his medical school days he paid very little attention to the claims of the Christian life. At the time of his marriage and during the first years of their married life he and his wife both were nonchalant about the Christian faith. Even at the time of the coming of their children they kept their accustomed ways. However, the children became old enough to play with other children who went to synagogue, to Mass, and to the nearest Holy Roller meeting in a polyglot downtown district near the medical school and hospital where the father was then a resident physician. The parents began to have to face the questions of the children about God, Christ, and the Christian way of life. This young doctor said that he and his wife came to a steadfast decision: " We got up off our all fours and went to church with our own kids. We began asking questions and trying to find out what all this talk about the Christian faith was all about, anyhow! " The turning of the heart of the father to the children paved the way for a fresh revelation of God.

Obedience and Authority Begin to Show

In the second place, God's sovereignty is revealed to the child in his parents' demands for obedience. Or, on the other hand, if the parents so provoke the child, they may by an unreasonable and inordinate desire to dominate the child obscure the knowledge of God from him. The apostle Paul puts it this way: " Children, obey your parents in the Lord, for this is right. . . . Fathers, do not provoke your children to anger, but bring them up in the discipline and instruction of the Lord " (Eph. 6:1, 4). For instance, our Lord himself, at the same time as he was " venturing out upon his own " at the Feast of Passover, nevertheless went down with his parents and " came to Nazareth, and was obedient to them " (Luke 2:51). In the larger context of Jesus' relationship to God the Father as "the only begotten Son," Jesus learned by the things he suffered and was "obedient unto death." How easy it would have been for his foster father, Joseph, so to have stood between the growing boy and his Heavenly Father as to have distorted the very character of God in the eyes of his son!

The groundwork for obedience to God is nurtured in the admonitions of a wise father who exercises a reasonable and loving degree of affectionate authority in the life of his child. Yet he does not so frustrate and limit the growth of the child that the child becomes discouraged. He is enabled to do this because he himself as a parent is subject to the sovereignty of God. He takes his stand alongside his child as a weak and sinful person, needing the guidance of the Heavenly Father. Herein is laid the basis for true democracy in the home and in society.

GROWTH CALLS FOR INDEPENDENCE

In the third place, children learn obedience in childhood. But under God their growth demands that they learn independence and self-direction as they grow older into adolescence and adulthood. Therefore, God's liberation of human persons from infantile bondage is made known to the young person as he learns to " leave his parents." Jesus pointed out that there are two reasons why a person should, in the fullness of his years, leave his father and mother. He leaves them emotionally and spiritually in order to be able to give his fullest devotion to God in Christ in the Kingdom of God. Spiritual growth is hindered and his vision of God obscured by remaining in the parental " nest." The wings of freedom are never flexed or tested in the risk of free flight as long as parents remain as one's idol.

Furthermore, such " leaving of parents " is necessary for

the experience of Christian marriage. Jesus said that for the sake of marriage "a man should leave his father and mother, and cleave to his wife; and they twain shall become one flesh." Yet negative evidence of contemporary life points to the way in which emotional immaturity produces confused religious perspectives and emotional incapacity in the institution of marriage.

Lewis M. Terman, in one of the earliest studies on the causes of marital unhappiness, found unmistakable evidence that maternal and paternal overprotection, resulting in emotional immaturity, was the most frequent source of marital unhappiness and incompetence. Evelyn Millis Duvall has recently studied the problems of in-laws and has, in her usual highly readable style, written a book entitled *In-Laws: Pro and Con* (Association Press, 1955), which points up ways in which some of the problems that Terman discovered can be wisely overcome. But suffice it to say here that the old Jewish wisdom of teaching the child the law of God and a way to earn his own livelihood by the time he is of age has real relevance for the spiritual maturity and marital success of our overprivileged as well as our underprivileged children in America today. Otherwise, the youth always remains a child and becomes allergic to responsibility either before God or in relation to his fellow man.

This kind of parental overprotection not only obscures and distorts the growing child's later relationship to a marital partner or to his work; in a grotesque sort of way it also does the same thing to the young person's vision and understanding of God. I was asked to confer with a young mother who had been admitted to one of our hospitals for psychiatric care. In addition to her medical problems, she was confused and doubtful of her faith in God. She had many questions about which she wished to talk with a minister. Her physician asked me to confer with her. When I encouraged her to express her questionings and doubts concerning God, she became quite fearful. She said: " In my home, religion was always a matter my father settled for us, and there was no questioning allowed. We would never have dared to express our doubts to our father." I pointed out to her that this was one of the main differences between God and her father. God could stand being questioned and her father could not. It is an act of real faith to bring one's doubts to God in face-to-face prayer. Likewise, she could never become a person in her own right before God as long as her father did *all* her thinking for her. One of the root problems that had precipitated her illness was the sudden death of her father. Sooner or later a child has to get along without his parents. Emotional disturbance really sets in if the parents leave all the adjustments of maturity for a child to accomplish when they, the parents, die. Early, then, the parents should encourage the child to have an autonomous relationship to God. The worship of God as a chief end of our existence not only glorifies him but also brings our own personhood to full-grownness.

The necessity for leaving one's parents puts a double load of responsibility upon them. In the tender years of a child's life, through sickness and health, parents center their lives upon the child. Pagan religious rites have often centered upon the sacrifice of children to gods. Christian family life has reacted against this offering up of the fruits of one's body for the sins of one's soul. To the contrary, Christians are most thoroughly tempted to become idolaters of their children, thereby both binding them to themselves and forsaking the claims of maturity as well. The child, in order to become a person in his own right, must rebel. He is faced with the dilemma of having to leave his parents without at the same time dishonoring them.

HONORING AND DISHONORING PARENTS

In the fourth place, in such a crisis as I have just described, the eternal God reveals his power to sanctify and mature a growing person in his command that we " honor our father and our mother." There are two ways of leaving our parents, one that honors them and one that dishonors them. The claims of maturity require that a growing boy or girl, in order to be a full-grown Christian and an effective marital partner, leave his parents. However, this leaving must be done in an honorable way. Young people honorably develop autonomy from their parents when they learn how to earn their own living, develop a clear-cut sense of vocation and calling under God and go out into the large family of mankind to do creative work in the Kingdom of God. Often they may have to do this with little or no encouragement from neglectful, indifferent, or even jealous parents. But regardless of this, the integrity of the growing child himself requires that he gain his independence of his parents in accordance with the will of God and thereby honor them.

The counseling pastor, and especially the college counselor of students, hears a poignant story of almost monotonous repetitiousness and sameness. Students who become behavior problems are often " getting back " at their parents for domination, neglect, deception, and exploitation of one kind or another. They are like Hamlet in his soliloquies, mumbling in their all too young beards about the jumbled and inconsistent relationships of their parents. They have often done things of which they are not proud, do not know what drove them into such senseless and irresponsible acts, and yet vaguely wonder if an undertow of resentment, desecration, and repudiation of their parents is not strangely connected with it somehow or other. Some of them even seize upon the real delinquencies of their parents as a whining complaint to justify their own loss of integrity before God and man. Many compulsive, driven, and unhappy young persons often cannot achieve autonomy from their parents without desecrating them. They do so by delinquent behavior, embarrassing incidents, or refusing to become self-supporting persons.

However, Christian wisdom was quick to see that this is the "first commandment with a promise." The person who achieves his autonomy from his parents through an honoring and edifying path of freedom enters into a fuller promise of the rewards of his labors. He has his parents restored unto him "a hundredfold now in this time." Contrary to much superficial popular psychology, religious convictions, activity, and calling are not always means of "conformity" to parents. Rather, religion may be a very real way in which a child rises up and becomes a person in his own right in relation to parents who are quite indifferent to or hostile toward spiritual matters. Here the child chooses the way of the Christian faith to rise up and "leave his father and his mother," to follow the Lord Jesus Christ. When he does so, if he is true to the whole of his faith, he always honors his parents, even in the act of rebellion.

The Care of Helpless and Aged Parents

Finally, God preserves human life as he lays upon children the responsibility of caring for their aged parents. Jesus pointed out to the Pharisees that they had a fine way of setting aside the commandments of God. He called their attention to the way they took that which they would have given to their aged parents and infirm parents, and gave it to the Temple instead. He scored the Pharisees heavily for using this exploitative way of getting new revenue for the Temple, and he laid upon his listeners the responsibility of sustaining and caring for parents in the helpless stages of their old age. One of the major social problems of today lies in the fact that the longevity of the average person's life has been increased by twenty years in the medical and social progress of this century. The insecurity of older people and the medical problems associated with old age have increased the admissions of elderly persons to mental hospitals by six times in the past thirty years. Many of these persons have in their earlier years neglected their children and in turn are being neglected by their children. On the other hand, many of them, after long years of faithful service to their children, are neglected by their children and left in someone else's care.

The poignant words of Jesus come to us again and lay this responsibility heavily upon our minds and hearts. Jesus himself at his crucifixion turned to his beloved friend and asked him to care for his (Jesus') mother. The subtle reminder of the commandment of God is that we are to do this in order that it " may be well with us." This awakens us to the fact that we too may not avoid the experience of old age and infirmity. God's purposes are revealed to us from generation to generation as we understand how he has divinely purposed that one generation should minister to another and in turn be ministered unto by that generation.

The truth of God is from generation to generation and from everlasting to everlasting. The unfolding cycle of the years reflects the fingerprints of God's concern for parents and children. The movement of the hand of his purpose and the strength of his mighty outstretched arm are made known to us in the intimate nuances of family life between parent and child. At each stage along life's way, at each turning in the pilgrimage of faith, and at each teachable moment of life's crises, God reveals himself to us and becomes known to us in the breaking of bread together in our own households.